Thinking it through

Also available:

Teaching Thinking Skills Across the Early Years
Belle Wallace
1 85346 842 8

Using History to Develop Thinking Skills at Key Stage 2
Belle Wallace and Peter Riches
1 85346 928 9

Thinking Skills and Problem-Solving – An Inclusive Approach
Belle Wallace, June Maker, Diana Cave, Simon Chandler
1 84312 107 7

Using Science to Develop Thinking Skills at Key Stage 1
Max de Boo
1 84312 150 6

Thinking in Literacy at KS 1
Paula Iley
1 84312 282 0

Thinking in Literacy at KS 2
Paula Iley
1 84312 283 9

Thinking it through

Linking language skills, thinking skills and drama

Gill Thompson and Huw Evans

 David Fulton Publishers

David Fulton Publishers Ltd
The Chiswick Centre, 414 Chiswick High Road, London W4 5TF

www.fultonpublishers.co.uk

First published in Great Britain by David Fulton Publishers 2005

10 9 8 7 6 5 4 3 2 1

David Fulton Publishers is a division of Granada Learning Limited, part of ITV plc.

Note: The right of the authors to be identified as the authors of their work has been
asserted by them in accordance with the Copyright, Designs and Patents Act 1988.

Copyright © Gill Thompson and Huw Evans 2005

British Library Cataloguing in Publication Data
A catalogue record for this book is available from the British Library.

ISBN 1 84312 190 5

Typeset by FiSH Books
Printed and bound in Great Britain

Contents

Accompanying CD

All lesson plans and resources are copied on to the accompanying CD for readers to amend if necessary and print out.

About the authors

Gill Thompson is currently the head teacher of a small rural primary school in Herefordshire. She has been involved in delivering courses for teachers and teaching assistants to support children with learning difficulties and communication disorders and has contributed to the LEA training courses for teachers, SENCOs and teaching assistants. She is also a qualified Speech and Language Therapist and has worked in France, the USA and South Africa as well as in England.

Gill is the author of *Supporting Children with Communication Disorders – A handbook for teachers and teaching assistants* (David Fulton Publishers).

Huw Evans is the head teacher of a Hereford primary school and is involved in initial teacher training and headship mentoring within the county. He has a special interest in raising children's self-esteem, encouraging the use of thinking skills throughout the curriculum and developing environmental awareness within the school setting. In 2002 he had a year's secondment as a KS2/3 Maths Consultant for the LEA. Huw visited Latvia in spring 2004 as a member of a team investigating teaching and learning styles and looking at provision for gifted and talented pupils.

Acknowledgements

This book has been a collaborative venture, made possible by the children we teach and the staff and students we work with. We are grateful to the writers of books, journals and articles that have informed our writing and to the leaders of courses and conferences who have reinforced the ideas presented in our writing.

We would also like to acknowledge the support and encouragement of our families.

Introduction

Teaching children to 'think' has now become an acceptable part of educational practice and the benefits of using activities to develop thinking skills are well researched. It is not, however, always possible to fit this into an already congested timetable and, along with drama and other creative subjects, it is often an occasional 'add on' rather than an integral part of teaching.

The three main methods that are used for developing thinking skills are

- through the delivery of a structured programme such as the 'Somerset Thinking Skills Course' which is timetabled separately from other subjects
- by using subject-specific thinking activities in science, mathematics or geography
- by a cross-curricular approach to teaching which promotes and encourages the development of thinking opportunities.

Language is the vehicle that we all use to reason things out and to process the information that constantly bombards our senses. We hold 'internal' conversations with ourselves as we mentally examine auditory, visual and kinaesthetic stimuli and make informed judgements based on our previous knowledge and experience. Both language and thinking are instrumental in sorting and classifying received data, sequencing, comparing and relating that data to previous knowledge and experience.

Young children are involved in the constantly evolving process of learning, developing the closely linked systems of language and thinking to help them make sense of their environment. Children who do not have well developed language skills find it difficult to fully understand received information and do not have the ability to question what they hear or to extend their thinking.

If we think of language as a box of 'tools' which enables us, not only to communicate with one another, but also to unravel the complexities of day-to-day problems, then it is clear that the better the 'toolbox' is equipped, the easier it is to sort out the problems. Similarly, the very process of looking at a problem from different aspects and being helped to think a problem through can introduce us to a wider language base. Children do not necessarily acquire these reasoning and thinking skills automatically and strategies for thinking need to be taught as part of the whole curriculum through specially designed activities, use of careful questioning, discussion and reflective dialogue. This necessitates an approach to teaching that provides children with the skills and opportunities to reflect and draw conclusions as they evaluate information, explore possible outcomes and make reasoned judgements.

Children often need to be encouraged to become better thinkers, to look beyond the

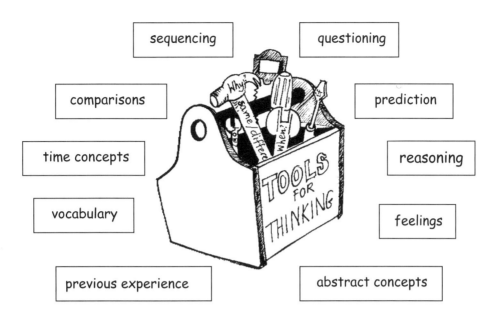

The Thinking Toolbox

literal and to make reasoned judgements. They do not, however, necessarily have the tools to enable them to process information, to reflect on the different aspects of a situation or to relate their own experience to problem solving. As teachers, we can help to provide the 'tools' for the 'toolbox' by promoting the development of receptive and expressive language skills, extending children's thinking, encouraging them to examine and investigate, and using the type of questioning approach that stimulates creative thinking.

The authors have worked together to provide a collection of practical ideas which incorporate thinking activities and drama into lessons across the curriculum. The activities are the result of first-hand experience and have been used successfully with children of different ages and abilities.

The following chapters include background information on the value of this approach, resources, examples of lessons and a framework for further lesson planning that any teacher can use or adapt without having to do a great deal of in-depth reading or preparation. The language skills that are targeted can be easily identified and could be part of the individual target-setting process or individual IEP objectives for pupils with specific language difficulties.

With the current emphasis on inclusion, teachers need to address an even wider range of ability within their classrooms and to plan accordingly. The lessons provided in this book are presented in a format which is easily accessible, can be quickly adapted for individual classes, shows National Curriculum links and also provides suggestions for differentiation and extension. Many of the suggestions could be used by teaching assistants when supporting individual pupils or groups of pupils, with the emphasis on questioning skills, language use and challenging children's thinking and learning.

1 Language and thinking

Language is the ability to understand and use a structured system of communication. It is a component of the whole process of learning and is essential for accessing every aspect of the school curriculum. If a child has a difficulty in understanding or using language, it is likely to impact on everything that they do, in every facet of their lives.

Language skills are fundamental to literacy development – they are the foundation that underpins understanding, speaking and listening, communication of ideas, reading and writing. Children can think more effectively as they develop the language skills to structure their thought processes but, conversely, the development of thinking strategies helps with the acquisition of language skills, allowing the teacher to model language structures that the child can put to a purposeful use. By encouraging a child to be actively engaged in a learning situation you are helping them to plan and guide their own learning.

A study in America by Goodlad and Sizer (1984) showed that education has traditionally relied on a high percentage of 'teacher talk' as opposed to active involvement by pupils. This does not encourage the development of language and thinking but promotes a dependence on accepting information at face value without questioning it.

> Where teacher talk is the main medium of transmission the child is effectively excluded from learning, to the frustration of both child and teacher.
>
> (Nash *et al.* 2002)

In the classroom children can be helped to observe, compare, contrast, predict, sequence and use evidence to support their points of view. They need to learn to differentiate between fact and opinion and to internalise their thought processes through language, examining relationships and drawing conclusions about observed behaviour. By valuing children's opinions and allowing them to discover things for themselves through questioning and experimentation we enable them to become more confident and more prepared to listen to and assimilate what others have to say.

> The better we are at interpreting the data and challenging the assumptions behind them, the greater our chances of handling the riddles, the conundrums and the paradoxes that are so prevalent. Questions make it possible.
>
> (Goodlad and Sizer 1984)

Early language development is linked with the development of cognitive, social and communication skills. Central to the development of language are the child's abilities to focus attention, to learn through play and to form social interactions. Research into child development indicates that children are in the 'acquisition' stage of literacy learning up until the age of 8 years and it is during these early years that a child's potential for developing reading skills and language processing are developed (Clay 2002). If we encourage a child in these early years of language acquisition they can be helped to make sense of the vast amount of sensory stimuli that invades their consciousness.

In order to comprehend the developmental process, it is useful to be aware of the initial stages of the normal pattern of speech and language development. This can only serve as a guideline, as every child progresses at a different pace, but it can demonstrate the basis of the acquisition of communication skills and the understanding of language concepts. It also demonstrates the extent to which other developmental areas, such as motor skills and cognition, influence the progress of speech and language development (see Table 1.1).

If we are aware of what language skills are expected at specific ages and the sequence of their development, we are better equipped to underpin and support the process and provide activities that encourage and enrich that development. As teachers we need to provide children with the tools to enable them to develop enquiring minds and to have the language skills to acquire, extend and use their knowledge and experience in a purposeful context, thus reaching their potential throughout the curriculum.

We need thinking in order to make even better use of information.

(De Bono 1993)

The lesson plans in this book (see Chapters 5 and 6) are designed to target specific language skills and concepts as well as providing ways of teaching strategies for looking beyond the literal and for questioning and processing information. Children need to draw upon their experience, recalling previous information, making links between objects, events and behaviours, making comparisons and looking for similarities and differences and predicting possible outcomes. They need to accept that it is fine to make mistakes and that there is often more than one correct answer to an investigation. Children need to learn, understand and use the language related to this type of activity so that they can order and plan their own investigations and thus promote further learning. If children apply their learning in this way, their skills are used in a relevant and creative way and are directed by the children's own desire to find out more.

Thinking activities

- **Comparisons** is a very adaptable teaching tool for lessons and reinforces the concept of exploring things beyond their literal presentation. Looking at two everyday objects and challenging children to find similarities and differences encourages them to look further and to investigate aspects of the objects that they would not normally bother with; and, by working with a partner or in a group, they use language to communicate their ideas that helps them to make sense of their findings. It can be used at the start of a project or at the conclusion. It can be used as a mental starter activity or as a plenary or stand on its own as a means of promoting investigation and discussion.

Table 1.1 Speech and language development

- **At the age of 1 year** the child responds to some verbal commands (such as 'give it to me') and attracts attention by using several 'words' which have a definite meaning. Understanding is developing at a faster rate than expressive ability as the child learns the names of familiar people and things but may not yet have the ability to say those words.

- **1–2 years** – In the course of the next 12 months the child begins to use words and gestures, uses 'inflected jargon' which imitates sentences but has little meaning to the listener, responds to simple commands and may refuse to do these by saying 'no'.

   The child starts to use familiar early phrases – ('bye-bye' 'all gone'), repeats single words that are said to him/her and asks for the toilet, food or drink.

- **At the age of 2–3 years** the child asks questions ('what's that?'), talks in simple terms about immediate experiences and repeats much of what is said to him/her. He/she refers to self by using a pronoun ('me go out', 'me want drink') and vocalises readily. Speech and language at this age are part of the child's 'egocentric' world where personal needs and the child's immediate environment are the focus of attention (Piaget 1959).

- **At the age of 4–5 years** the child increasingly communicates through speech and carries on long involved conversations. He/she can tell or re-tell a story, although this may be a mixture of real and imagined events, and is eager to find out how things work and what things mean. This is the age when children ask a lot of questions although they do not necessarily understand the explanations. The child is beginning to socialise more with other children and an increase in the child's linguistic development occurs around this age – sentence structure is now sufficiently complex to allow the child to describe and abstract experiences, and vocabulary develops as the child becomes increasingly interested in listening and taking in information. He/she begins to use these skills to internalise thinking. The child begins to 'think' words as they are uttered and to develop a process of 'planned' speech as he/she moves from egocentric speech to more mature communication.

- **Between the ages of 5 and 6 years** the child begins to develop an understanding of temporal concepts and learns to see things from another's point of view. He/she starts to use language as an instrument to make judgements, to analyse and categorise and to draw on previous experience to inform actions and decisions. The rate of development and understanding of language concepts will have a direct influence on the child's ability to think things through and make sense of the world around them.

Source: based on developmental profiles by A. Gesell, J. Lindon and C. Hood in Gesell 1966

- **Questions** can be adapted to a variety of curricular activities and, once children have learned to ask questions out loud, they will begin to formulate their own questions when they approach new situations and new concepts. This helps to structure their internal thinking, using the language of questioning and the knowledge that by asking questions you find out more and more.

> There have always been plenty of questions in schools, but most of them have come from the teacher, often at the rate of one question every 2–3 seconds. Unfortunately, these rapid fire questions are not the questions we need to encourage because they tend to be RECALL questions rather than questions requiring higher level thought. The most important questions of all are those asked by students as they try to make sense out of data and information. These are the questions which enable students to Make Up Their Own Minds.
>
> (Postman and Weingartner 1975)

- **Hot seating** is a drama technique that has a place in most areas of the curriculum. A child can take the 'hot seat' and respond to questions about something he/she knows well or can take on another role and answer questions from a different perspective. The questions themselves are ways of probing and stimulating responses and children will quickly learn how they can phrase their questions to get the most effective and informative responses.
- **What's my picture?** is another activity that can be adapted to different groups of children and different subjects. The skills involved can be differentiated according to the age and ability of the children, and the selected pictures can be related to the lesson being taught or to the vocabulary objectives of a literacy, numeracy or science lesson.
- **Barrier games** are infinitely adaptable and can be as simple as a sequence of six coloured cubes or as complex as a detailed structure or picture involving shapes, colours, positioning, patterns, etc.
- **Let's find out** is an activity that can be done with any picture that has the potential to tell a story – again it involves questions and discussion about what the children see and can relate to their own experience and encourages them to go beyond the superficial image and look for clues to a more detailed and exciting story. This is a good way to start a topic. If the children have some idea of what they want to know, they can plan a learning journey to follow and then set about their investigation in a methodical way, taking charge of their own knowledge acquisition. The lesson or project can conclude with sharing what they have actually learned and how they achieved this knowledge.
- **Thinking quiz** – this is a good way of motivating a class, stimulating discussion and producing ideas for further development. The results of the quiz can be plotted into a mind map, which can then be used for individual story or poetry writing, collaborative writing or creative artwork. The quiz questions can be written to reflect a specific theme or lesson objective.
- **'Jungle Adventure'** and **'Space Voyage'** give children the opportunity to become involved in an imaginary situation and then to talk about their experiences. This

can be the stimulus for a creative writing task or stand alone as a speaking and listening activity.

- **'My friend says…'** is a circle activity that encourages listening, recall and communication skills. The teacher can direct the focus of the activity according to the group of children, their age and ability or the theme of the lesson. The outcome will be useful as an informal observation/assessment opportunity or as a way of introducing the skills of careful listening and retelling information.
- **'What is it?'** is a simple drama game which develops imagination and concentration and provokes thinking. It can be adapted for younger or older children and can be done with an object, articles of clothing or a piece of furniture. Put a chair, for example, in the centre of the circle. The children take turns to mime an activity, changing the chair into another object, e.g. television, cupboard, car. The others have to guess what the chair has become.

> We never stop investigating. We are never satisfied that we know enough to get by. Every question we answer leads on to another question. This has become the greatest survival trick of our species.
>
> (Morris 1967)

2 | Thinking skills

Being a good teacher involves being concerned, not just about the teaching that happens in the class, but also about the pupils' learning. Although the two terms are often used together, good teaching does not always produce good learning and sometimes children will learn even though the teaching is poor. If 'thinking skills' is to be introduced into a class/school then it is vital that it involves both 'teaching' and 'learning'. A teacher needs to know what strategies are needed to develop the skills and the pupil should be provided with a range of skills to help in the learning process.

Teaching *skills* rather than *content* is becoming more alien in education. The current National Curriculum is very content-driven and therefore it is worth pausing for a while to consider the concept of teaching 'skills'. One simple way to understand this would be to use eating fruit as an example (Figure 2.1). You can learn that to eat an apple you can eat the flesh and skin but usually leave the core. Once you have this knowledge you could apply it to eating a pear but not a banana. So you learn another fact – to eat a banana you have to peel it, not eat the peel but eat the flesh. Now that you have this new knowledge you can apply it to a few other fruits possibly, but not all. Learning the skill to eat an item of fruit would be to think about what you need to know – 'Is the skin tough or bitter?' If so don't eat it, discard any hard seeds, etc. Equipped with these skills of analysing, evaluating, deciding, etc. you can then have a good go at eating any fruit! A silly example but hopefully it makes the distinction clearer.

Figure 2.1 How to eat different types of fruit

The Royal Society of Arts (RSA) came up with a competence (skills)-led school curriculum in its publication *Redefining Work* (RSA 1998), and further expanded and defined this in its publication *Opening Minds – Education for the 21st Century* (RSA

1999). They wanted to focus on educating children for the world of tomorrow and not today. They based their work on the belief that the country is not thinking hard enough about how to prepare young people for the knowledge society, where change is a permanent feature. Employers are looking for, but not finding, people who know how to manage themselves in a range of situations, who can recognise problems and how to resolve them, who know how to 'communicate'. Young people recognise those requirements too. They don't want a 'one size fits all' curriculum but one that meets their own needs and connects to their own lives.

The competence-led framework starts from a different set of principles to that of the curriculum teachers and pupils are used to. It expresses what pupils should *learn from* their education, not what should be *taught to them*. It is not described in terms of subject material or organised subjects. It does not prescribe any particular content. The content is seen as primarily the medium through which pupils should develop competences. There are five broad categories, of which we will mention two, showing how they link into the teaching of thinking skills:

Competence for learning

- pupils have learned, systematically, to think

Competence for managing information

- pupils have developed a range of techniques for accessing, evaluating and differentiating information and have learned how to analyse, synthesise and apply it.

But what is 'thinking skills'? You can easily find packages currently available for schools on thinking skills which suggest that, if bought, they would cover what you need to introduce the subject to the class and school. There is a growing range of these packages and the better ones state that the teaching of thinking skills is a *process* and cannot simply be slotted in as a separate entity. It is the process we wish to focus on in this chapter and, through looking at what needs to be covered and how it can be covered, you will see that thinking skills can be incorporated into any lesson.

There are many definitions of thinking skills. The National Curriculum (1999) states that 'By using thinking skills pupils can focus on "knowing how" as well as "knowing what" – learning how to learn' – and lists the key skills as

- Information-processing skills
- Reasoning skills
- Enquiry skills
- Creative thinking skills
- Evaluation skills.

It is the focus on 'how to learn' that is most important. Thinking skills is about giving children the ability to choose for themselves what type of thinking they need at different times. This therefore involves the teacher setting up plenty of opportunities within the class for the children to be challenged into using the range of skills, but the children also need to be able to label the skills. One well-known method of labelling thinking is De Bono's 'thinking hats'. Each coloured hat is associated with a type of thinking, (the hats can be real or imaginary) e.g. the white hat would be linked with information and facts – what you need to know and where you would get that knowledge from; the red hat would be feelings – intuitive and instinctive thinking. There are six hats altogether and children would be encouraged to use them all when faced with a problem to solve, etc.

Costa and Kallick (2000) state that research has shown that there are some identifiable characteristics of effective thinkers. They call them 'habits of mind'. These are patterns of thinking and behaving in intelligent ways. Table 2.1 lists the sixteen 'habits of mind' along with some of the authors' suggestions for a simple way of getting the children to understand what those characteristics are. These can be used in a poster form in the classroom to encourage the children to remember and use them.

Another simple framework for adults in the class to keep in mind, as a way of monitoring the kind of thinking expected by the pupils, is Costa and Kallick (2000) 'six process categories':

- Remember
- Understand
- Apply
- Analyse
- Evaluate
- Create.

To enable the children to have opportunities to practise the 'habits of mind' and other thinking skills strategies, classroom management and in particular the teaching approaches within the class need to be carefully thought of. Developing the skills of 'thinking' happens more readily in an ethos of respect and challenge. The main things to consider would be:

- adult–pupil interaction, especially questioning
- pupil–pupil interaction: group and paired work
- format of the lesson.

When considering these three things, it is important to ensure that pupils have the opportunity to talk. They need to develop technical language, they need to discuss and they need to listen to other pupils' opinions and answers. Talk is so important as a stimulus to thinking and as a means of moving thinking on. Talk – speaking and listening – should not be restricted to English and drama lessons. It is just as important in other subjects too.

Children need to talk about the mathematics they are learning. Talking helps children to put their ideas into words. It makes them think about the mathematics they are doing.

When they explain, children make their own ideas clearer to themselves. They get used to using new words. They understand things better.

(*Assisting Numeracy* 1998)

Table 2.1 Habits of mind (after Costa and Kallick 2000)

Habits of mind	
Persisting	Stick to it!
Managing impulsivity	Take your time!
Listening with understanding and empathy	Understand each other!
Thinking flexibly	Look at it another way!
Thinking about your thinking (metacognition)	Know your knowing!
Striving for accuracy and precision	Check it again!
Questioning and problem posing	How do you know?
Applying past knowledge to novel situations	Use what you learn!
Thinking and communicating with clarity and precision	Be clear!
Gathering data through all senses	Use your natural pathways!
Creating, imagining and innovating	Try a different way!
Responding with wonderment and awe	Have fun figuring it out!
Taking responsible risks	Venture out!
Finding humour	Laugh a little!
Thinking interdependently	Work together and learn from others!
Remaining open to continuous learning	Learn from your experiences

Each new idea in mathematics involves the children in learning in three areas – linguistic, conceptual and procedural. The children learn in that order. This means that if the children are unsure of the language of maths they will not understand the concept and, as a result, they definitely will not be able to do anything with that concept. For example, when learning about shape, words such as quadrilateral and even triangle can be difficult for some pupils. Taking the time to make a link between those words and something the children already know is important to enable them to use the words appropriately. By linking triangle to tricycle and quadrilateral to quad bikes they then have that link which will result in learning. Remember also that even simple words, that may seem not worthy of any time to explain, could cause confusion; e.g. the word 'right' (as spoken) could mean:

- opposite of wrong
- opposite of left
- 'yes'
- 'immediately'
- the verb 'to write'
- 'feeling fine'
- 'accurate'
- the size of an angle.

This highlights the importance of spending time on addressing the linguistic aspect of maths learning and ensuring that the children have grasped the correct meaning of the language and vocabulary.

Listening is equally important. Many children learn more from their peers' explanation of a concept than they would from an adult's, so it is essential to fit in a time within lessons for children, either individually or in groups, to explain how they did their work, found out the answer or tackled a challenge. Listening is also important for the adult. So when you listen to the children talk about their learning it is the ideal time to find out about what they have understood and what misconceptions, if any, they are forming. You can also use these times to get them to think things through carefully by explaining more clearly what they meant.

Questioning skills

Using good questioning skills can be a stimulus for improving children's use of language and for developing higher order thinking skills. The effective use of questioning can have a major influence on children's learning and could take up a book in itself.

Points to remember:

- A question should make connections and not restrict thinking. Using open questions as well as closed questions is vital. A closed question would have just one correct answer whereas open questions would have a number of different correct answers. A simple example is:

Closed question: What is 2 x 6? There is only one answer, which is 12.

Open question: What two numbers could you multiply together to give 12? Several answers are possible, 2 x 6 being one of them. But you can also accept 3 x 4, 1 x 12 or even 24 x ½. Already you can see that it is much easier to include differentiation with open questions and you are more likely to involve all the pupils.

- A question should involve all pupils. Adults in the class should be wary of choosing the same children to answer. Do not always choose the children with their hands up, choose the reluctant ones – draw them in, or even better use individual whiteboards so that all pupils can answer at the same time.

- A question should be appropriate to the task and to the pupils learning. Some questions are fine for using as a method of summative assessment, enabling you to find out what the children have learnt, e.g. 'What are the months of the year?' 'Who wrote the "Harry Potter" books?' Others stimulate the children in thinking about how they came to learn what they did, e.g. 'How did you decide who the main characters were in the book?' 'How did you find the answer to that word problem?'

- Questions should be used to support children in their learning

    When the children are getting started with a piece of work:
    'How are you going to tackle this?' 'What do you need to find out?'
    Making positive interventions to check progress:
    'Can you explain what you have done so far?' 'Could there be a quicker way of doing this?'
    When the children are stuck:
    'Can you describe the problem in your own words?'
    'Can you talk me through what you have done so far?'
    During the plenary session:
    'How did you get your answer?' 'If you were doing it again what would you do differently?'

    (Adapted from *Mathematical Vocabulary* (1999), where you will find more of these types of questions and a useful explanation of closed and open questions.)

- Questions should be followed by an appropriate '*wait time*' to allow for a response. A six-year investigation in the USA during the 1970s observed thousands of lessons which were all transcribed and the mean 'wait time' (the time teachers allowed between them asking a question and the children answering) was measured. Amazingly this came out as only 0.9 seconds (Budd Rowe 1999). This low wait time suggests that only a few of the children could possibly be quick enough to answer and many must be completely left out of the interaction. When the investigation went on to encourage teachers to increase the wait time the following effects were noted:

    - The children gave longer, more involved answers
    - More children joined in
    - The children showed increased confidence of response
    - They challenged or improved the answers of some of their peers
    - More alternative explanations were offered.

This is definitely worth a try!

? ? ? ? ? ? ? ?

Spending some time thinking about what questions to include in the lesson is a good use of planning time. Questions can be the driving force of the lesson. There is no need to write down all the questions but just the key ones. Many published schemes do this now, but remember – *you* know your children best and you know where they are with regard to their learning and whether the set questions are appropriate. Some questions can occur spontaneously as a result of discussion with the class and it is always a good idea to write down the best ones for future reference.

Another good suggestion to try when children answer questions is to pair them up so that they can have a brief discussion before answering. Pairs could be of similar ability or a brighter child could support another who finds expressing ideas more difficult. There are many obvious benefits of using an 'answer buddy', not least the linguistic development already mentioned.

Many of the ideas discussed, to work efficiently, will rely on a more flexible classroom management: one that values the children as learners and one that recognises that not all children are the same in their learning styles. If we consider, for example, two types of learning style – the *inchworm* and the *grasshopper* – and how that applies to learning maths, it is possible to focus on the most likely types of thinking each personality would use. This would allow us to work out what sort of apparatus would benefit the learners best. (See Table 2.2.)

Table 2.2 Inchworm and Grasshopper (after Chinn and Ashcroft 1993)

Inchworm	Grasshopper
Personality	
Prescriptive nature	Intuitive nature
Analytic	Holistic
Finds formulas	Forms concepts
Looks at facts	Estimates
Has recipe for solution	Uses controlled explanation
Writes down	Solves inside head
Unlikely to verify	Likely to verify
Tends to use + and −	Tends to do × and ÷
Apparatus	
Number lines	Dienes blocks
Multilink	Cuisenaire rods
Counting blocks	Graph paper and grids
Unifix cubes	Geoboards
Paper and pencil	

■ Differentiation

Continuing on the theme of classroom management and involving all the pupils in learning and developing their skills in thinking, it would be useful to look at the underachievers. This group will not necessarily be on the Special Needs Register although, as a result of their frustrations and lack of achievement, behaviour problems and lack of motivation can easily manifest themselves if their needs are not addressed early enough. Teaching the skills of thinking to this group will equip them with the tools to help them access the content-heavy curriculum and learn from one another through discussion and investigation.

It is also worth mentioning other ways to support these children. According to Barbara Prashnig (1998), underachievers have seven key learning styles and needs:

1. Mobility at frequent intervals
2. Variety of learning tools, resources and teaching methods
3. Informal seating arrangements in the learning environment, because of their inability to sit on hard chairs for more than 10 to 15 minutes.
4. Low light because their brains seem to get over-stimulated, especially by fluorescent light, which often leads to agitated behaviour
5. Tactile/kinaesthetic learning tools and resource materials to introduce new and difficult material through their preferred modalities because they are not usually highly visual or auditory
6. Non-authoritarian teachers who treat these students collegially and know how to respect their nonconformist thinking
7. Recognition of their high motivation, despite their obvious problems, which are often caused by inappropriate teaching methods.

3 Drama and thinking

Drama is invaluable as a means for developing language skills, encouraging social interaction and group participation and teaching children how to listen and respond appropriately. It is a multi-sensory tool, which combines listening, speaking, thinking, exploration and use of the immediate environment and the development of physical control.

> Whether studied as a subject in its own right or as a learning medium across the curriculum, drama makes an important contribution to pupils' progress in school.
>
> (Arts Council 1992)

Drama can be used within the context of other subjects as a method for exploration of facts or relationships or to enhance understanding. It can be a means of focusing a child's experience and putting their learning into a realistic context. Drama can broaden children's understanding of concepts, develop their use and understanding of language and provide memorable creative experiences which can be drawn on in future problem-solving situations.

There are a variety of drama techniques that lend themselves to creative thinking and can be used to develop language skills:

- Role play
- Hot-seating
- Puppetry
- Improvisation
- Freeze frames
- Circle games
- Memory games
- Storytelling
- Debating
- Mime

These techniques can be used as units in their own right or as a part of the curriculum to help reinforce specific areas of a lesson, to explore an aspect of learning or to enhance and enrich the quality of learning about historical, social or moral issues.

A picture, photograph or object can be used as a stimulus or starting point for developing roles or situations. A piece of music or a story can inspire improvisation and development of characters, settings, and situations. A piece of improvised drama can become a focus for discussion and a means for children to communicate ideas. Children should also be able to explore the expressive possibilities of their voices and bodies through structured activities and improvisation.

Through drama, the teacher can encourage children to contribute their own ideas, thoughts and feelings based on experience or a willingness to explore further. Children who find the writing and recording of lessons difficult often find that they can achieve well in the less restrictive environment of a drama session and can recall facts and events through having experienced them or having watched others recreating a scene.

The lesson plans provided in this book can be adapted to all aspects of the curriculum and should not be restricted to literacy lessons. 'Acting out' a situation enhances the child's recall of facts – this can relate to science, history, geography, RE, PSHE, numeracy or project work. Language skills are used through group interaction and the need to express and share ideas. Specific areas of language development can be targeted and reinforced through these lessons. Suggestions for language/speaking and listening objectives are included in the lesson plans but can be adapted to suit the individual children in your class or for the area of the curriculum being used.

Lesson ideas

- Using a familiar story as a basis for developing questioning skills can be very rewarding. If you were to use the story of 'Cinderella' and discuss the characters and the situation initially, allowing the children to think of the sequence of events and details of the story, then the children could become newspaper reporters and plan questions to ask the neighbours living around Cinderella and her family:

    Does Cinderella get along with her step-sisters? Are they a happy family? Have you noticed anything unusual going on recently? Did you hear noises last night? Did you see a coach and horses in the yard? Are they a friendly family? How long have they lived in the house? Did you see Cinderella returning home late last night? What time was it? What was she wearing? etc.

    They could act out the interviews in groups and then use the responses to write a report for a newspaper. A similar activity could be done for other traditional stories.

- Characters from a variety of stories could meet at a party and be introduced to each other – what conversations would occur between Little Red Riding Hood and Snow White, between Goldilocks and Prince Charming or between the wolves from 'The Three Little Pigs' and 'Little Red Riding Hood'? A selection of picture cards featuring characters from well-known stories is a valuable resource for all sorts of activities and can be the starting point for collaborative or individual work.

- Use sections of a historical picture such as the Bayeux Tapestry and create a freeze frame tableau – then bring it to life with each character playing their role. Encourage the children to think about the character's work, status, relationship to the others and how they would feel. They could be given cards with written questions or the following ideas could be written up on the board:

    When did they last eat? What did they eat? How long have they been at sea?
    Which one of the other characters is their friend or enemy? Do they get seasick?

Is the Captain a tyrant? How does he punish or reward the crew? How does it feel on board ship with all the horses and other animals? How does it smell? Where do they sleep/wash/eat? How were they enlisted to work on board ship? Have they left friends and family behind? Do they miss them?

They could ask each other the questions, as if having a conversation with a fellow-worker. After this, the children can respond to questioning by the teacher or other children – they should answer keeping in role. This may sound challenging but has been successfully done on many occasions with children from Reception to Year 6 and with a class of children with special educational needs. You will be amazed by the detail and ideas that develop from this type of activity.

■ Puppets are always popular, especially with younger children, and can be a great way of encouraging questions. Introduce the puppet and tell the children that something happened to the puppet last night – they can each ask two questions to see whether they can find out what occurred. They must listen to each other so that they do not repeat the same questions:

Where were you? What were you doing? When did it happen? Was it dark? Where were you going? Who was with you? Were you meeting someone? Was it a good thing or a bad thing that happened? etc.

■ Science topics such as magnetism, the water cycle, weather, forces, life cycles, etc. can be acted out to show the sequence of events, symbols used or the movement style. This type of dramatic re-enaction can be used as part of a class assembly to demonstrate ideas to the rest of the school.

■ Geography topics can be developed through drama with children acting out stories, lifestyles, traditions and situations from other countries or planning journeys and transport, comparing different environments or exploring recycling and environmental issues, presenting news bulletins or weather forecasts.

■ PSHE offers possibilities to improvise conflict situations such as playground disputes, bullying, being lonely, cheating, school rules, stranger danger, road safety, etc. and to encourage children to think how it feels to be in these situations and how they would respond.

Children need to develop an understanding of the boundaries between pretence and reality and, in this present age of technological toys and games, they need the opportunity to engage in imaginary roles and situations. Drama offers them a way of stepping into the shoes of another character and finding out what it feels like to be in a different situation where they will need to develop strategies for dealing with the problems that arise.

The shared experiences and engagement in role play and acting help pupils to develop the essential language skills of speaking and listening.

(Line 1997)

4

Assessment and planning

Assessment

In each lesson plan we have included learning objectives related to the lesson content and assessment criteria. You may wish to add individualised targets for your lessons or for individuals – these will be dependent on the particular children in your class and their learning styles and needs.

Targets and objectives should be

- Specific – clear, unambiguous and easy for the children to understand. Giving children a written set of basic success criteria will prompt them to keep to the given task and can suggest vocabulary to be used, ways of developing or extending the task and reminders of how they can make their work even better.
- Measurable: set targets that allow you to make an assessment that provides evidence of progress, e.g. children will use the language of contrast and comparison appropriately, children will use questioning to extract useful information from their partners, children will respond creatively to questions about a story character using appropriate language and staying in role, James will recall details of his partner's holiday and retell them to the class.
- Achievable – specific aims that can be realistically achieved by each class member with suggestions for extension for the more able.
- Relevant: children should feel that the task is being done for a reason or their motivation will suffer – it could be based on what they have decided *they* want to find out, related to their own individual learning targets, or could be shown to be part of an investigation that will be celebrated by a display or presentation. Discuss the relevance of the activity when you introduce it to the children and they will understand why they are doing it and what the end product may be.
- Timed: if you set a timescale for the project – 'by the end of this lesson/ next week we will need to look at your findings', 'the newspaper report will be printed on Friday', etc. – the children can work within set time boundaries and can be encouraged to pace their work appropriately.

You can assess informally using verbal feedback and observation of the way children are interacting, using their language skills, learning and using the vocabulary, and being self-motivated and on task. You may wish to record your observations so that you can monitor progress and achievement.

It is useful to take photographs or use a video recorder as a means of keeping a visual record of the children and their work. This acts as valuable evidence and is a record that the children themselves can use for self-evaluation as well as for the sheer pleasure of recalling the various activities. Older children can use photographs to develop a display or book, writing captions, speech bubbles or more detailed accounts of the work undertaken. Photographs or video clips can be incorporated into a PowerPoint presentation or Talking Book as part of an ongoing project.

By setting lesson objectives and targets for assessment, you will be able to monitor the progress the children make and will see how language skills are successfully developed and used through this approach.

Planning your lessons

Effective teaching relies on effective planning but it does not have to be onerous. The document *Excellence and Enjoyment: A strategy for primary schools* (DfES 2004) heralds a long-awaited, more realistic central government view on planning. A central message of this document is that teachers have the power to decide how they teach and that the Government supports that power. This allows a greater freedom for teachers to be more creative with their lesson plans and is an ideal opportunity to focus more on developing the skills for thinking. If you want further evidence that over-detailed lesson plans are a thing of the past read on.

> Planning is an essential aspect of teachers' work. All teachers need to plan what they will teach and how they will teach it . . . no prescribed form or length.

All that is specified in the Ofsted framework is that:

> Teachers plan effectively, using clear objectives that children understand.

> Time should be used for aspects of planning that are going to be useful for their own purposes and which have a direct impact upon the quality of teaching and learning.

> Collaborative planning can be liberating, supportive and effective.

> The National Literacy and Numeracy Strategies though they are supported strongly, are not statutory and can be adapted to meet schools' 'particular needs'.

The document also mentions where the next area of development is going to be with regard to the National Numeracy Strategy and the National Literacy Strategy:

> The next steps to support Literacy and Numeracy will be –

> Literacy

> - Securing the place of speaking and listening both as a key foundation for literacy and also as an essential component of all effective learning.

> Numeracy

> - Encourage pupils to become numerate thinkers
> - Apply their knowledge and skills to solve increasingly complex problems
> - Use mathematics to reason and explain.

What better endorsement can you have to encourage you along the lines of developing the children's language and thinking skills?

Teaching the skills of thinking is basically employing the principles of good teaching. Practically all the strategies and suggestions given in this chapter to develop children's thinking skills can equally be applied to developing their learning in other areas. Through adopting the strategies and the style of teaching mentioned in this chapter, and developed further in other parts of the book, you will also be addressing, for example, creativity. Creativity involves:

- curiosity – having an enquiring mind
- flexibility – lateral thinking and making connections
- willingness to think the impossible
- confidence to try things out
- ability to handle uncertainty
- perseverance in the face of adversity
- self-reflective awareness.

All of these are developed through teaching children the skills of thinking. By opening the children to a range of thinking strategies you also address some of the needs of the gifted and talented children, allowing them to move further. That movement isn't necessarily linear; children don't have to take on the content of the year above to be challenged. They can move sideways, looking at a problem in greater depth, considering all avenues and coming up with, maybe, some unexpected conclusions.

Lesson format

In the following two chapters we have suggested two possible planning formats for you to use, which will hopefully simplify your planning and can be made compatible with the system used in your school. As we have indicated in Chapter 2, there is a move towards using a simpler and more manageable planning format and some schools are accepting 'mind maps' or similar visual planning sheets as working documents.

- The headings within the templates are intended to help you see how these lessons meet the National Curriculum requirements and year group NLS/NMS targets but are there for you to use as it suits you.
- We have suggested which age groups the lessons are appropriate for but, with some adaptation, you may decide to use them with younger or older pupils.
- Suggestions for questions to incorporate into the lesson are intended as a prompt – there are likely to be a range of other questions that you will find relevant. Try to use open questions and encourage the children to listen to each other's responses.
- The listed outcomes within the 'lesson evaluation' box are useful reminders and could be ticked or annotated, to be used for future planning.
- You will find that these lessons can be used over and over again with the same children just by changing the subject matter. The overall process improves with practice, developing your confidence and the children's ability to apply their thinking constructively. The language concepts and vocabulary become embedded in the children's general communication skills with regular application and can then be monitored as part of the assessment process.

5
Literacy lesson plans

The following lesson plans have been used with different age and ability groups and are intended for you to adapt and personalise to suit the needs of your own class. The literacy lessons are intended to develop language skills and speaking and listening through drama and thinking activities. Language skills and thinking skills are interdependent in that they both provide a scaffolding for the development of one another, but they are also essential components of the wider learning journey and impact on every aspect of the teaching and learning curriculum (Figure 5.1).

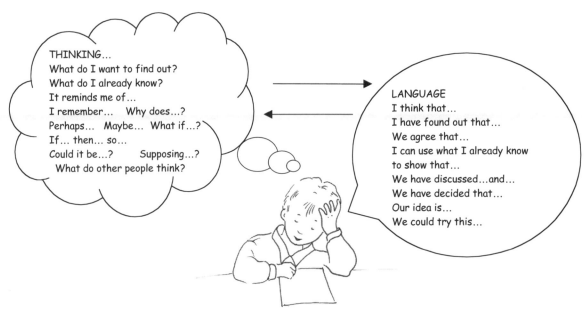

Figure 5.1 Language and thinking

LESSON 1   Contrasts and comparisons

Most children accept things at face value and do not investigate or question without prompting. By asking them to look at two items and identify the similarities and differences we are encouraging the children to embark on an investigation, looking for clues and examining familiar, everyday objects with fresh eyes. As a by-product, they will begin by using the language skills that they already possess and develop and use the target vocabulary and language related to the activity.

Working with a partner offers the opportunity to share ideas through visual and tactile experience and to translate this into verbal information. This can be further developed by asking one pair to share their findings and ideas with another pair before presenting their work to the rest of the class.

This lesson plan (A) takes two books as the items for comparison. It has been used successfully in a variety of contexts:

- Two books that are different versions of the same story by the same author, *The Owl Who Was Afraid of the Dark*, by Jill Tomlinson, in paperback version and picture book version
- Different books by the same author, e.g. *The Worst Witch* and *Peace At Last*, by Jill Murphy
- Books sharing a similar topic but fiction/non-fiction, e.g. *The Hodgeheg*, by Dick King Smith, and *The Life Cycle of a Hedgehog*
- Different text genres – narrative, poetry, play script, diary, information, etc.

Any two books can be selected for this activity, even different editions of the same book.

The activity takes the language of the literacy hour further and provides a stimulating opportunity for children to examine books in detail without asking them to 'read' fluently or write in more than note form. It then encourages them to interpret their own data and present it verbally. New vocabulary and language can be introduced and modelled and can be presented as a word-bank or set of example phrases.

The lesson plan offers opportunities for development and modification to match the age and range of abilities of your class and to link to your planning objectives. It can be used as a 'starter' task to introduce a new text or text genre, it can be used at the end of a week of work to build on the information that has been taught, or it can be the basis of a literacy project.

Extension/differentiation

Less able children can be provided with a ready-made grid and a vocabulary bank and their recording can be very simple. Adult support can be used to encourage and guide the investigation. The grid and word-bank can be used in Clicker 4 format for pupils who find writing difficult.

More able pupils can be asked to design their own grid, possibly using Venn or Carrol diagrams, or to write their information in more detailed sentence form.

ICT could be incorporated to draw the grid, sort and display the information and interpret the data further. The Comparisons chart can be used on an interactive whiteboard and children can record their observations as part of a whole class activity.

Variations

The activity is not only suitable for use with books. In numeracy, two numbers can be investigated, looking for similar and different features – odd/even, greater than/less than, multiples of, factors of, number of digits, size of font, style of font, etc.

Objects or shapes can be used for comparison – number of faces, edges, corners, 2D/3D, size, colour, more than/less than, regular/irregular, etc. (see Numeracy lesson plan 5: Shape).

This can be used successfully as a 'plenary' activity, consolidating work covered in the lesson and providing assessment opportunities (see 'Same and different,' p. 64).

The range of possibilities extends to other curricular areas, examining and comparing pictures of costume, habitat, environment, etc. or contrasting information in history, geography and science.

LESSON 2   Hot Seating

This drama activity gives children the opportunity to use their imagination and step into the footprints of a well-known character from a familiar story. They will have some prior knowledge of the character from their previous contact with the story but they can then let their own ideas take over and the story can develop in a totally original direction. The children who ask the questions are taking on the role of investigative reporters and need to think of questions that will give them more background information on the story. They will elicit responses that will show the story from a new point of view. The activity will vary each time it is carried out, depending on the individual children, the way the situation is set up and any prior focus that is created. It can generate ideas for extended writing, for a collaborative class project, or for character studies, or it can be used on its own as an enjoyable 'thinking' activity that takes the children beyond the pages of a story book, bringing the original tale to life.

This lesson plan (B) takes the story of 'Little Red Riding Hood' but could be adapted for any story book characters. It has been used successfully in RE, History and geography with children from both KS1 and KS2. The Three Little Pigs, Cinderella's father, Florence Nightingale, the Prodigal Son, a Victorian child and a child from an Indian village have all been hot seated with memorable results.

Sitting in the hot seat

Follow-up work has included a set of 'wanted' posters for the wolf, a complete newspaper dated the day that the Three Little Pigs' houses were burned down, the wolf's version of the Little Red Riding Hood story, alternative stories based on Cinderella and her family, Noah's Ark log book, descriptive writing about the life of children in Victorian times and a diary from an Indian village.

Extension/differentiation

Less able children can be provided with prepared questions or be helped to devise their own. Adult support can be used to encourage and guide the investigation. They could be helped to record the responses to their questions to aid recall for later use or the interviews could be recorded on tape. More able pupils can record the interview and write it up as a newspaper report, thinking up a headline and planning the structure of the report according to set guidelines.

Work can be word-processed and a publishing package can be used to organise the articles. PowerPoint can be used to create a presentation based on the role play.

Variations

This activity can be repeated many times with different characters and the children will become more proficient at devising questions and being in the hot seat, with practice and familiarity.

The teacher can take the hot seat and direct the story to provide encouragement for the questioners or another adult can visit the class 'in role'. This has worked well in a Reception class when the tiger from *The Tiger Who Came to Tea* visited and helped the children to make a shopping list for his needs and proved to be a friendly beast who just wanted a caring home!

LESSON 3   Questions

Children often find it difficult to use the question words in a constructive way and need help to develop questioning skills that will help them find out more about an object or a person or a story.

The words can also present difficulties with reading and spelling for younger children and you may need to give them some 'tricks' to help them remember which word is which:

WHAT?   'What is that hat on your head?' Encourage the children to visualise a really absurd hat with fruit or birds or strange shapes. Tell them that the word 'hat' is hidden in the word 'what' and they should imagine that strange hat when they think of the word.

WHERE?   'Where did you put your book?' 'Here...' – the smaller word 'here' could be the answer to 'where?' and can be a prompt for recognising or writing the word.

WHY?   – it sounds like the letter 'y' – don't forget the 'h'!

WHEN?   'When will the hen lay her egg?' – picture a hen and an empty eggcup – 'hen' is hidden in the question word.

WHO?   'Who made that noise? A Wise Hooting Owl...teaching mnemonics for short words is a good way to start this spelling strategy

HOW?   'How will you get there? Hop Or Walk?' – act out the actions and talk about other ways of 'getting there' but emphasise that to remember this word you need to think of hopping and walking.

Keep a set of question word cards (see Figure 5.2) close to hand that can be used at the beginning of a lesson or as a plenary activity – distribute the cards to selected children and encourage them to think of a question to ask beginning with their word. This could be done when introducing a new book, a picture, a puppet or book character, a visitor to the class, a topic, or a concealed object.

Lesson Plan A – Literacy: Comparing books (1)

	Year group/s:
	Years 3/4

Learning objectives/lesson focus: Comparing books. **NC targets** - Yr 3 term 1, T 17, 18, 19, 20, term 2, T 13, 17, term 3, T 8; Yr 4 term 1, T 16, 17, term 2, T 23.
The children will investigate similarities and differences and use the appropriate language to discuss and record their findings. They will extend their use of related vocabulary. They will be more observant when picking up a book in the library.

Targeted language skills: the vocabulary of comparison, vocabulary related to the activity, discussion skills, oral presentation.

Resources: Each pair of children should have two different books, a worksheet each, pencil/pen, vocabulary card on each table.
Teacher - two different books - these can be books by the same author, a fiction and a non-fiction book, a picture book and a reading book, a story book and a poetry book.

Vocabulary: same/different, similar, more/less, bigger/smaller, thicker/thinner, author, illustrator, illustrations, pages, contents, index, chapters, font, prose/poetry, rhyme, barcode, price, information, fiction/non-fiction, audience, cover, blurb, title, style, paper, card, soft-back/hardback, shiny, coloured, setting, character.

Whole class work: The children should sit round in a circle. Show them two different books and a chart on the board for recording similarities and differences. Encourage the children to suggest what features of both books are the same – the shape (rectangle/square?), the materials it is made of, the fact that they both have a title, a blurb on the back, etc. Then ask them to suggest differences. Record their suggestions on the board, modelling sentences or phrases. Explain that they are to work in pairs to record their own findings about two books.

Group activities: Each pair will discuss their two books, looking for similarities and differences. They will record their observations on the worksheets and use the vocabulary card if necessary to help them write sentences.

Differentiation: Less able children may need support to work in a pair or to write their observations. Where appropriate, the child could use single words or simple phrases or use an adapted worksheet using cloze sentences. It may be necessary to enlarge the worksheet to A3 if the child has large writing or poor vision, to rule lines and/or to stipulate a specific number of same/different features to be found. More able children can be given books that match their interest/reading level. They could work without the vocabulary card. They can design their own chart.

Plenary: Pairs of children should present their findings verbally, deciding who should read the similarities and who the differences.

Lesson evaluation:
Were the children engaged during the introduction?
Were they able to suggest relevant similarities/differences?
Were they able to present their findings clearly and sensibly?
Did they work well in their pairs?
Did they complete the task successfully within the time allocated?

Lesson Plan A – Literacy: Comparing books (1)

Before the lesson

Make sure that resources are prepared.

How does this lesson relate to previous work covered?

Share your plans with the teaching assistant. Prepare observation sheets or discuss specific support tasks for the teaching assistant to do. (Observe how a particular child contributes to the group activity, listens and responds, uses the targeted language, engages with others, manages behaviour. Use additional cues, word cards, explanations.)

Language

Ensure that children understand the related vocabulary and can use it appropriately – same/different, similar, more/less, bigger/smaller, thicker/thinner;

author, illustrator, illustrations, pages, contents, index, chapters, font, prose/poetry, rhyme, barcode, price, information, fiction/non-fiction, audience, cover, blurb, title, style, paper, card, softback/hardback, shiny, coloured, setting, character.

Resources

Each pair of children should have two different books, a comparisons worksheet each, pencil/pen, vocabulary card on each table.

Teacher – two different books – these can be books by the same author, a fiction and a non-fiction book, a picture book and a reading book, a story book and a poetry book, etc.

The comparisons chart can be enlarged as a poster or presented as part of a flip chart on the whiteboard.

Questioning/thinking

Use 'open' questions that have a range of possible answers...

How are the book covers different?

What things are the same?

Are the shape, size, colour, materials the same? If not, what is different?

Look at the inside of the books – what features are alike? How can you tell? How do you know?

What makes you say that?

Year group 3/4

Learning objectives/lesson focus:

Comparing books – investigate similarities and differences

Targeted language skills: language of comparison

Vocabulary	same/different, compare, similar, alike, more/less, bigger/smaller, style

Introduction: Show two different books and encourage children to suggest how they are similar and different.

Whole class work: Record children's suggestions on the board, modelling sentences and phrases.

Group activities: Children work in pairs to compare and contrast their 2 books. They record their observations on the chart.

Differentiation: Support for specific groups/individuals to aid recording of observations (tape recorder, scribe, multiple-choice sheet, word-bank).

Plenary: Pairs of children present their findings verbally.

Outcomes: Did the class complete the given tasks successfully? What did they learn?

Lesson evaluation/assessment

Were the children engaged during the introduction?

Were they able to suggest relevant similarities/differences?

Were they able to present their findings clearly and sensibly?

Did they work well in their pairs?

Did they complete the task successfully within the time allocated?

Lesson Plan B – Literacy: Hot seating (1)

	Year group/s: KS1/KS2

Learning objectives/lesson focus: Hot seating
NC targets – text level work on role play, character, social/cultural/moral issues, changing point of view.
The children will recall the traditional story of 'Little Red Riding Hood'. The characters will be discussed and then one child will be selected to play the part of the woodcutter. The other children will play reporters and ask questions. (With very young children, the teacher can go into role.)

Targeted Language Skills: speaking and listening, questioning skills.

Resources: A story book of 'Little Red Riding Hood'.
A newspaper to look at report format.
A piece of costume or a prop to help woodcutter get into role.

Vocabulary:
Question words – who, what, when, where, why, how
Vocabulary related to the story.

Group activities: The children should work with a partner or in a small group to decide what questions they should ask the woodcutter – they can be helped to formulate questions e.g. Where do you live? What did you hear? Had you seen the wolf before? What were you doing in the wood? Did you see the little girl walking through the wood? Have you ever killed a wolf before? Where do you think the wolf came from? Did you know the girl's granny?

Whole class work: The woodcutter should sit in the 'hot seat' and be prepared to answer the questions from the class. He or she can be briefed to give some ideas (perhaps the wolf had escaped from a zoo, there could have been a reward offered to anyone capturing the wolf: the woodcutter could be a policeman in disguise looking for robbers: he may not have killed the wolf but captured it to return it to a safari park...)

Differentiation: Less able children may need help to ask questions. Where appropriate, the children could have help from a teaching assistant. More able children can be encouraged to ask more in-depth questions or could be selected to sit in the 'hot seat'.
Extension: Different children can be called on to 'hot seat' as different characters – the Granny, Little Red Riding Hood's mother, Little Red Riding Hood herself, her schoolteacher.

Plenary: The story can be re-written on the board using the reporter's information. This could lead to a piece of extended writing in the form of a newspaper report.

Lesson evaluation:
Were the children engaged during the explanation of what to do?   Did they plan appropriate questions?
Were they able to ask their questions and listen to other 'reporters'? Were they able to speak with confidence and clarity?
Did the child in the 'hot seat' respond well and use his/her imagination?

Lesson Plan B – Literacy: Hot seating (2)

Before the lesson:

Read or tell the story of 'Little Red Riding Hood'.

Talk about the different versions of the story and how there are variations.

Discuss the setting and the character of Little Red Riding Hood – is she a shy, quiet girl or a confident, cheeky girl who does not do as she is told? Discuss the character of the woodcutter.

Model some possible questions that would provide useful information.

Resources

Story book or story poster.

Chair.

Individual whiteboards and markers or pencil and paper.

Follow-up activity – write a newspaper report with headline, picture and caption.

Language/drama

Select a child to sit in the 'hot seat' and play the part of the woodcutter.

Other characters for the 'hot seat' could be the Granny, Mother, Little Red Riding Hood herself, the wolf, Little Red Riding Hood's teacher, next-door neighbour or school friend.

The rules of the activity are:

one question at a time is asked;

children must give time for the response;

everyone should listen and take notes of the responses.

Learning Objectives/lesson focus	Year group
Targeted language skills – questioning skills	
Resources	Vocabulary
	Words associated with buildings and materials
Whole class work	
Group activities	
Differentiation	

Questioning/thinking

The person in the 'hot seat' must try to stay in role...

What time did you leave your house? Do you always work in this forest?

Where were you going?

Did you know there were wolves in the forest?

Where do you live? What did you hear? Had you seen the wolf before? What were you doing in the wood? Did you see the little girl walking through the wood? Have you ever killed a wolf before? Where do you think the wolf came from? Did you know the girl's granny?

Outcomes/assessment

How well did the children use questions to find information?

How well did the child in the 'hot seat' stay in role and respond to questions?

Did the children find the activity difficult?

Which questions were best for giving information?

Did they listen to each other?

Did the follow-up work reflect the information from the hot seating session?

what	where
?	which
who	when
why	how

Figure 5.2 Question word cards

LESSON 4 'My friend says'

This is a very adaptable activity, which the children enjoy and which will demonstrate how the skills of listening and then retelling information develop and progress with practice. The lesson illustrated (C) is intended for the beginning of term when the children have been on holiday. It can, however, be used in a wide variety of contexts and is an ideal activity for Circle Time.

The discussion focus could be:

- my favourite/least favourite food
- pets
- ideas for improving the playground/school
- things that scare me
- how I would spend £100
- what I want to be when I grow up
- hobbies
- a school visit – feedback – the part I liked best/least
- TV programmes I like and why.

Lesson Plan C – Literacy: 'My friend says'

	Year group/s: KS1/KS2

Learning objectives/lesson focus: Listening and communicating information

NC targets – pupils learn to speak confidently and listen to what others have to say. PoS English

The children will work in pairs around the circle, listening to what their partner tells them and then reporting back to the circle.

Targeted language skills: speaking and listening

Resources:
An object to pass around the circle – a shell, pebble, soft toy etc.

Vocabulary:
Holiday-related vocabulary.

Whole class work: The children should sit round in a circle. The rules of circle activities should be revised – only the person holding the pebble (shell, toy, etc.) can speak, the others must listen. When a child speaks to the circle they should speak clearly so that everyone can hear what they have to say. Explain that they will start by working with the person sitting on their right side. They will take it in turns to tell their partner about a recent holiday, how they got there, who went, the best thing that happened, etc. Their partner must listen carefully.

Group activities: Each pair will take turns to tell their partner about their holiday. It is important for the listening partner to listen well as they will later relate their partner's holiday story to the circle.

After a set time to exchange stories (about 3–5 minutes) the pebble is passed around the circle and each child should tell their partner's holiday story.

Differentiation: Less able children may need support and prompting to listen, recall and retell the story. Where appropriate, the children could have help from a teaching assistant. More able children will naturally recall greater detail and the expectation of their account should be higher.

Plenary: Pass the pebble around again and encourage each child to say a word related to holidays. As the pebble moves around the circle, each child must recall the word from the previous circle members as well as adding a new word.

Lesson evaluation:
Were the children engaged during the explanation of what to do?
Did they listen well in their pairs?
Were they able to retell their partner's story? Were they able to speak with confidence and clarity?
Did they adhere to the 'circle' rules?

The children are given the subject for discussion and take it in turns to share their comments with their partner. They then tell the group what their partner said. This is a good opportunity to encourage them to listen and recall and to then put the information into the correct sequence verbally. Initially some children may find this difficult, but they will become more at ease and more proficient as the activity is used regularly.

The children's ideas can be recorded and used as data in a chart or mind map. A child can be selected to do the recording. The data can be used to inform subsequent written work, as part of a research project or as the starting point for further discussion in PSHE.

LESSON 5 'What's my picture?'

Buildings can be described in a wide variety of language categories – shape, size, colour, materials used, purpose, simile, position and location, etc. When introducing this lesson (D), depending on the age and ability of your class, you may wish to provide suitable vocabulary and examples of questions that the children could ask.

The idea of the activity is for the children to work in pairs and for one child to use questions to find out information about the picture of a building. If they use closed questions, the information provided will be limited to a 'yes' or 'no' answer but if they ask more open questions they will find out much more and their partner will be able to provide more descriptive answers.

'Is it somewhere that people go to do something special?' ('People go there on Sundays and for weddings and to sing.')

'Is it an old building or a modern building?'

'Is it made of stone or brick or wood?'

'How many windows can you see? What shape are they? Are they in the middle or at the sides of the building? Are they all the same shape and size?' etc.

When they feel that they have found out enough detail, they start drawing the picture and this will prompt more questions as they find out what they have not asked and need to know.

At the end of the session, explain that the object of the activity was to find information and is nothing to do with their ability to draw. How easy did they find it? What sort of questions did they ask? How helpful was their partner?

The lesson has been aimed at a class of children in Years 2 and 3 but could be adapted to younger or older children by varying the complexity of the pictures. The pictures could be of everyday objects; you could give the questioner a simplified black and white version of the picture and they have to ask about the colours of different parts of the picture and add details; the pictures could be of well-known buildings such as Big Ben, the Eiffel Tower, local landmarks etc.; they do not have to be limited to buildings and could be Christmas cards, postcards, story characters or fantasy creatures with strange and wonderful features.

Lesson Plan D – Literacy: 'What's my picture'

	Year group/s: Years 2/3

Learning objectives/lesson focus: Questioning for a specific purpose
NC targets – Yr 2 S6, S7, T 14; Yr 3 T9, T17
The children will work in pairs to use questioning skills to extract information about a picture of a building. They will use this information to draw a picture of what they think the building looks like. They will extend their use of related vocabulary.

Targeted language skills: the vocabulary of questioning, vocabulary related to the activity – positional language, size, shape and colour vocabulary, discussion skills, oral presentation.

Resources:
Each pair of children should have a postcard size picture of a building, pencil/coloured pencils, paper.
Teacher will need several larger pictures of buildings.

Vocabulary: high, low, wide, narrow, wood, brick, stone, window, door, roof, tile, slate, chimney, tower, square, rectangle, circle, on, under, next to, over, in, behind, floor, how many, how tall/short, what is beside it?

Whole class work: The children should sit round in a circle. Show them some pictures of different buildings and discuss the features – number of windows and doors, purpose of the building, materials used in building, shapes, sizes, etc. Explain that they are to work in pairs and one person will have a picture that the other cannot see. The person who does not see the picture is to ask questions to help them draw a picture of the building. Discuss the type of question that would be useful for providing information. The pairs of children can then begin the activity.

Group activities: Each pair will work together with A asking questions and B responding. When A has gathered enough information, he/she can start to draw a picture of the building. A must not see the picture.
When the drawing is completed it can be compared with the original.

Differentiation: Less able children may need support to work in a pair or to draw their picture. Where appropriate, the children could have a simplified image based on basic shapes. More able children can be given more complex images that match their ability level – a postcard of a local building or a famous building such as the Eiffel Tower or Big Ben.

Plenary: Pairs of children should present their pictures and discuss the activity and how they found it. What questions were best for providing information? How were they presented? How helpful were the responses? Did the pictures resemble the originals? How could the questions have been used to make the information more accurate?

Lesson evaluation:
Were the children engaged during the introduction?   Did they work well in their pairs?
Were they able to suggest relevant questions?   Did they complete the task within the time allocated?
Were they able to use the questions and answers successfully to find out what the building looked like?

LESSON 6   Barrier game

This is another activity that encourages cooperation with a partner while helping children to focus on the importance of giving clear and relevant information. It is possible to buy 'barriers' for this type of activity but an upright folder is just as effective. Children should sit opposite one another with the barrier between them. Both children start a blank five by five grid and one colours in the squares using red, blue, green and yellow crayons. Their partner should not see what they have done. When the grid has been completed the child gives verbal instructions to their partner to tell them which squares to fill in and which colour to use. Neither child should look at their partner's grid until the second grid has been completed. Children should compare their pictures and see if they were given correct information. Sometimes they will have produced a mirror image of the original or have confused left and right or top and bottom.

The activity can be made more complicated by using a larger grid and a wider range of colours. It can be varied by providing a picture rather than a grid or a pattern of objects, e.g. a set of 10 clown faces or 10 cars. Another variation could be to use coloured interlocking cubes and make a tower of 6 cubes – the second child is given instructions for duplicating the tower.

You may introduce the activity by giving the instructions yourself and then showing the children your own picture for comparison – this could highlight any children who have difficulty following the instructions and need more help.

LESSON 7   Jungle adventure

This is easier to do in a large space such as the school hall or out in the playground. (See Lesson Plan F.) Present the children with the scenario that they are going on a journey into the jungle and will have to encounter several difficult situations. Ask the children what sort of challenges they might have – swamp with crocodiles, fierce animals, snakes, spiders, rivers to cross, bridges over high gorges, rocks to climb, tunnels to crawl down, ruined temples, hostile natives, etc.

The children need to be divided into teams of approximately six. Their first team activity is to prepare for the journey – what equipment will they need to take? (tents, knife to hack down vegetation and for protection, food, water, camera, first-aid kit, etc.). They need to organise the team, deciding who takes what and what role they play in the team (photographer, hunter, archaeologist, doctor, etc.). Give the children about five minutes to get themselves organised and act out the preparation.

Each team should then sit down and you ask individuals about their team role and what they are carrying – they should respond 'in role'. You can adopt a role yourself – tour organiser, newspaper reporter, consular official warning them of the dangers – this will add to the atmosphere and fire the imagination. Explain that the teams must work together if they are to survive the journey and help each other. They should decide on one of their team who will get into difficulties and will need help – perhaps they get injured or are frightened of snakes/heights/dark places, etc.

Provide each team with a simple map, detailing various hazardous areas (see Figure 5.3 on p. 34). Then each team can set off on their journey. Observe the way they

Lesson Plan E – Literacy: Barrier game

Before the lesson:

Explain the process to the children – one child fills in the five by five grid using the colours red, blue, green and yellow. Show a completed grid and talk about how the children could give directions to someone else about filling in an identical grid – encourage them to suggest strategies and language to use – they could use coordinates or they could use terms such as left/right/, up/down/across.

Emphasise that the children will work in pairs and should not see what their partner is doing.

Language

Square, top, bottom, row, column, coordinates, number, letter, up, down, along, left, right, above, below, beside, next to, red, blue, green, yellow

Questioning/thinking

The child giving the instructions should decide on a strategy for giving the information and think how best to communicate clearly. They may decide to tell their partner to number the squares or they may work systematically row by row or column by column. They need to convey the system to their partner and give sufficient time for them to colour in the squares.

Resources

Blank five by five grids.
Coloured pencils or pens.
A barrier or folder to use as a screen.

Learning Objectives/lesson focus	Year group
Targeted language skills – questioning skills	
Resources	Vocabulary: Words associated with buildings and materials
Whole class work	
Group activities	
Differentiation	

Outcomes/assessment

How well did the children give instructions?
How well did the child behind the barrier respond to instructions?
Did the children find the activity difficult?
Which strategies were best for giving information? Did they invent their own systems?
Did they listen to each other? Were they able to work cooperatively?
Were the completed grids identical?

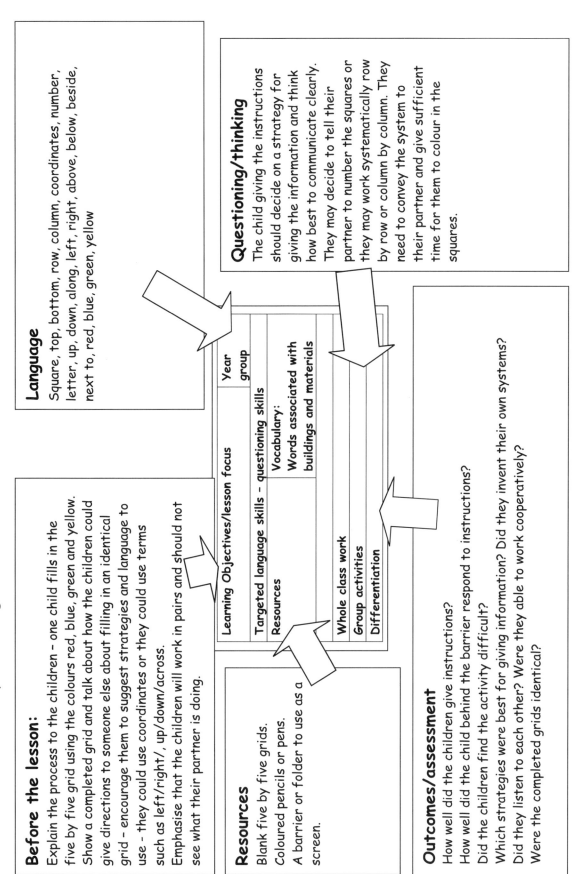

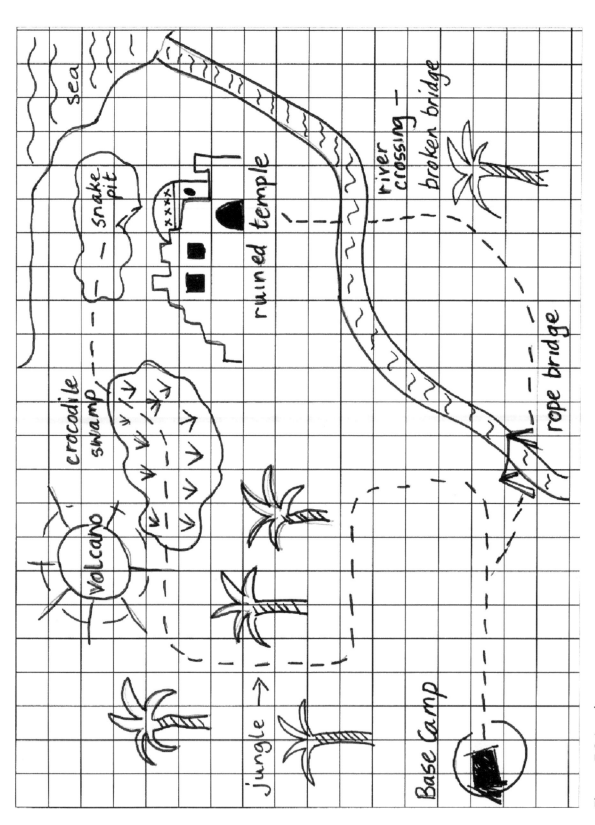

Figure 5.3 Jungle map

cooperate and support each other. When they reach the end of their journey they must make camp.

Ask individuals from each team to describe how they managed, how they overcame the dangers, what was the most unpleasant or frightening part of the journey, what they discovered, etc.

This activity can stand alone or be the stimulus for story writing or for planning work on an adventure holiday. Follow-up work could be done on lists (what equipment did they need?), maps and coordinates, countries that might have jungle areas, sequencing (write the order of the things you did on the journey – perhaps using a writing frame to plan), writing rules, investigating famous explorers, etc. The focus can be varied by making the journey an adventure on a planet up in space.

LESSON 8   Thinking quiz

Giving the children a quiz requires them to listen to the questions and think up responses. They need to understand that there are no right answers and it will be exciting and interesting to find out how different people have come up with different ways of answering the questions. (See Thinking quiz sheet.)

LESSON 9   Let's find out what has just happened...

There is a wide range of picture packs of paintings by famous artists available which can provide resources for this activity (Lesson Plan G). You may have access to pictures on a CD-ROM or you can download them from the Internet, showing them on an interactive whiteboard or overhead projector. Select a painting that has people, animals and buildings represented in the picture. Talk with the children about what they can see, seeking out fine details, facial expressions, clothing, tools, types of building, setting, etc.

The children should then work in groups of three or four to talk about what they think has happened just before the picture was taken or painted. (Where have the people or animals come from? What time of day is it? Were they working or at home or eating a meal? Were the children at school?) They could use speech bubbles to think of things that the people are saying or have just said.

Each group should choose one person to voice their ideas and share them with the rest of the class. Ask for the reasons behind their ideas – are there clues in the picture? why did they decide these things?

The activity can be followed up by arranging children into the positions of the people in the picture in the form of a tableau. On a given signal, the picture must come to life with the children improvising what will happen next and keeping in role.

This has possibilities for an investigation in art or history and could be developed into a larger project, reproducing the picture in the style of the artist, drawing and painting the characters and arranging them in a different setting, using a digital camera to take a picture of the children recreating the picture and then adding speech and captions or more detailed written work. It has possibilities for use as a Christmas assembly or performance or for a geography project based on an Indian village scene. Pictures can be found in magazines or text books or in the fiction library.

Literacy lesson plan F: Jungle adventure

Before the lesson:

Explain the process to the children –
They are going on a journey into the jungle and will have to encounter several difficult situations. Ask the children what sort of challenges they might have – swamp with crocodiles, fierce animals, snakes, spiders, rivers to cross, bridges over high gorges, rocks to climb, tunnels to crawl down, ruined temples, hostile natives, etc. What will they need to take with them?

Resources

Working space such as the school hall.
Map.

Language/drama

They need to organise the team, deciding who takes what and what role they play in the team (photographer, hunter, archaeologist, doctor, etc.). Give the children about 5 minutes to get themselves organised and act out the preparation. Each team should then sit down and you ask individuals about their team role and what they are carrying – they should respond 'in role'. You can adopt a role yourself – tour organiser, newspaper reporter, consular official warning them of the dangers. They then work in teams to follow the map and make the journey.

Questioning/thinking

Teacher asks questions of the adventurers –
What did you carry in your pack?
Were there snakes?
Which part of the journey was the hardest/most dangerous?
Did you have to help anyone or be helped?
Who was the group leader?
Were you worried at any time?
Why are you on this expedition?
Is it your first time?
Do you carry anything to protect you?
Is there anyone you wish to send a message to?

Learning Objectives/lesson focus	Year group
Targeted language skills – questioning skills	
Resources	Vocabulary Words associated with buildings and materials
Whole class work	
Group activities	
Differentiation	

Outcomes/assessment

How well did the children respond to the interviews?
Did they communicate well with each other during the adventure?
Did the children find the activity difficult?
Did they listen to each other? Were they able to work cooperatively?
Were they able to talk about the journey as if it had really happened?
Did it help with written work – diary writing, letter home, descriptive writing?

THINKING QUIZ

1. Think of 3 things that begin with the letter 'm'.

    ....

2. Think of 3 things that have a lid.

    ....

3. Think of 3 things that are green.

    ....

4. Think of 3 things you might find on or near the playground.

    ....

5. If you could invent a robot, what 3 things would you make it do?

    ....

6. If you could be an animal, what animal would you be and why?

    ....

    ....

7. Write 6 things you can buy at the supermarket.

    ....

8. You wake up one morning – how will you decide what
    clothes to wear for the day and what sort of weather it will be?

    ....

    ....

Name: .... Today's date: ....

Literacy lesson plan G: Let's find out

	Year group: Year 2

Learning objectives/lesson focus: Investigating the detail of a picture

Targeted language skills: question words, question format, past and future verb tenses, facial expressions, clothing, action words, etc.

Resources: Painting by L.S. Lowry – *Street Scene*, copies of the painting for each group, (http://www.l-s-lowry.co.uk) blank speech bubbles to stick to the picture.

Vocabulary: how, what, where, when, before, after, next, might, could have, might have, possibly.

Introduction: Show a copy of the painting on an interactive whiteboard/projection screen or give out several copies of the picture for children to look at. Ask the children what they can see – how many people/children? Where are they? What could they be doing? Where are they going? Are they all going to the same place?

Explain that there are no right or wrong answers – it is up to individuals to make their own minds up.

Main lesson:

Divide the children into groups of 3 or 4 and give them the following questions to respond to :

Where have the people/ animals come from? What time of day is it? Were they working or at home or eating a meal? Were the children at school? Are they going to watch something, go to market or are they on their way to school/ work….or something else? What time of day is it/What time of the year is it? Are there family groups or groups of friends? Who knows who?

The groups should decide on a 'story' for the picture and prepare to tell their story to the rest of the class.

They should use the speech bubble blanks, decide which of the characters are speaking and what they are saying to each other – the speech bubbles can be stuck to the picture.

Differentiation: Certain children may need encouragement/support to contribute to group discussions.

Help may be needed to organise the speakers for the presentation.

Plenary: Groups will present their ideas about the picture and explain their reasons.

Children could take up the positions of the main characters and, at a given signal, come to life speaking to each other – this could be extended into a follow-on drama session looking at relationships/outings/shopping.

Lesson evaluation:

Were the children engaged during the explanation of what to do? Did they listen well to each other in their groups? Did they use clues from the picture to inform their ideas? How well did they present their ideas? How well did they use their speaking skills to explain themselves?

6 | Numeracy lesson plans

Using thinking skills in numeracy encourages children to make connections between the skills and strategies they have learned and the real life problems that they will encounter. If the children start with investigations that are carefully structured they will develop the confidence to use this approach when undertaking relevant everyday investigations that they can relate to and see the value of. The children will have the opportunities to share their ideas, discuss what they already know, what resources they will need, what they plan to do, what works best, how to show their findings and whether they agree on their conclusions. The 'thinking' approach promotes the use of mathematical language and emphasises the learning that comes from trying different methods and making mistakes.

LESSON 1 Decimal maths

This lesson is aimed at Year 5 pupils and focuses on investigating decimal numbers that total 1 or 10. It uses Loop Cards as a mental starter and Target Boards for the whole class activity and for the subsequent group work.

Resources associated with this lesson and its variations can be found in the Resources section of the book and on the CD-ROM:

- Add and subtract vocabulary cards (p. 67)
- Target Board for calculations to 100 (p. 68)
- Blank Loop Cards (p. 69)
- One-place decimal Loop Cards (pp. 70–73)
- Target Board for addition and subtraction (p. 74)
- Target Board for adding to multiples of 1 (p. 75)
- Target Board for dividing into tenths (p. 76).

Numeracy lesson plan 1: Decimal maths (1)

	Year Group/s:
Learning objectives/lesson focus: *Calculations with decimals.* **NC targets** - Yr 5. The children will investigate decimal numbers that total 1 or 10. They will extend their use of related vocabulary. They will investigate patterns and relationships between number bonds to 10, 1 and 100.	Year 5

Targeted language skills: the children will develop the vocabulary of addition and subtraction through discussion of tasks and through creating word problems.

Resources: decimal loop set, decimal target board as OHT and as sheets for use by the children, whiteboards and pens, coloured counters, tenths template, blank target boards, vocabulary cards.	**Vocabulary:** decimal, digit, tenth, hundredth, decimal point, total, sum, add, increase, subtract, minus, decrease, difference, number bonds.

Mental maths: Each child will be given a loop card. The teacher starts the loop by reading the decimal and the child with that decimal represented numerically stands up and reads their decimal and the loop continues.

Whole class work: The children are shown the target board showing the decimals. The children are asked to read three examples to ensure understanding. The teacher then points to one of the numbers and the children have to work out what number needs to be added to make ten and write their answer on their whiteboards, e.g. the teacher could point to 5.5 and the children write 4.5. One child is chosen to explain the strategy used to work out the answer. This is repeated for five more numbers.

Group activities: Each pair will use the target board as a game to find the pairs of numbers adding to 10. Different coloured counters can be used to cover the pairs found. The work is then differentiated as follows:

Differentiation: Less able children should write all the number bonds to 10. They should then use the template provided to work out the number bonds to 1. They can cut out templates if required. They should discuss what relationships they notice between the two sets of number bonds.
The middle group can design a new target board on the same pattern as the original but using different decimal numbers, making sure that they include the pairs that add to 10.
The more able children should design a target board using totals to 1; they can use hundredths.

Plenary: using some of the numbers from the target board and the vocabulary cards, the children are asked to come up with questions they could ask, e.g. if the number 7.2 is selected and the vocabulary card 'decrease', a question could be 'What do you need to decrease 7.2 by to get 5?'

Lesson evaluation:
Were the children engaged during the introduction?
Were they able to participate in the mental maths?
Were they able to make links between different number bonds?

Did they work well in their pairs?
Did they complete the task successfully within the time allocated?

Numeracy lesson plan 1: Decimal maths (2)

Before the lesson:

1. Make sure that the resources are prepared with regard to the needs of your class.

2. Some previous work on number bonds to ten needs to have been carried out. If some children still find these difficult then reinforcement of these bonds should be the focus of their differentiated work but they should also have access to the number bonds to 1 (one decimal place) so that they can see the similarity in pattern.

3. Share the plans with the teaching assistant.

Resources

Decimal loop set – see pp. 70–73 for ways of using this.

Target board – make sure that children who have difficulties in reading tables from afar are given copies. Dyspraxics will need their own copies. The target board can be laminated for children and/or TA to play pairs. Tenths template can be copied on to card and children can manipulate the pieces to create a visual interpretation of fractions of a whole in their head.

The vocabulary cards can be given as homework, used as the week's spellings. Copies should be given to autistic children. They can also be adapted with the use of a Language master.

Language

The language surrounding decimals need to be shared and analysed with the pupils. Some of the brighter children can link 'deci-' to ten and this can then be linked to tenths. Decimals should be referred to as decimal fractions so that children make the link that decimals are part of a whole. Tenth and hundredth should have visual links, i.e. 1/10 and 1/100, but examples should not always be one hundredth or one tenth.

Learning Objectives/lesson focus	Year group
Targeted language skills	
Resources	Vocabulary
Mental maths	
Whole class work	
Group activities	
Differentiation	
Plenary	
Lesson evaluation	

Questioning/thinking

The biggest stumbling block for most children in understanding decimal fractions is the place value concept. Washing line activities where children have to physically place the decimal fractions help some children, particularly the visual and kinaesthetic learners, in understanding.

Useful questions to check understanding would be is *nought point one the same as nought point ten?* This allows children to consider whether when counting up in 0.1's that the number after 0.9 is 0.10. How many 0.1's are there in 2? 20? *Can you see a pattern?* This helps with the place value understanding. The activities in the plenary stretch the child's thinking beyond simply sequencing the decimal fractions.

Outcomes/assessment

Use the plenary to assist with assessment. The children who you are certain are confident in their understanding can be the ones who are stretched to come up with the questions. Then use the questions created to select other children you want to assess. Select the children according to the questions, e.g. if the question is decrease 0.4 by 0.1 you could choose one of the children in the lower group.

LESSON 2 Multiplication

This is a lesson plan aimed at Year 6 pupils and looks at multiplication, the associated vocabulary, and its relationship to addition and division. It also encourages the children to solve mathematical problems or puzzles, recognise and explain patterns and relationships, generalise and predict. The children are given the opportunity to discuss the calculations and the strategies that they will use to work them out.

> Resources for this lesson:
>
> - Bingo Cards (p. 77–82)
> - Ideas Bingo (p. 83)

LESSON 3 Factors

This is another lesson aimed at a Year 5/6 class, which looks at the operation of multiplication and the associated vocabulary, and its relationship to addition and division. This activity uses a multiplication square and the children play games using multiplication tables.

> Resources for this lesson can be found in the Resources section of the book and on the CD:
>
> - Complete the multiplication grid (p. 84)
> - Multiply and divide Loop Cards (pp. 85–6)
> - 'Which table am I?' (p. 87).

LESSON 4 Handling data

The main focus of this lesson is to allow the children the opportunity to relate what they see on the graph to what is actually happening. This understanding will not only help them in interpreting graphs but also in checking the correctness of graphs they will draw. They are given graphs as a discussion point and can think around them, considering what each part of the graph is telling them.

Questions should always be directed at helping them to relate the positive slope to something increasing and the negative slope to something decreasing. They should also be guided by use of questions as to the labelling of the axes and why it is important that this is standardised. 'What would have happened to our graph if the gaps between the points were not the same?' 'Would we be able to understand it as clearly?' Some of the more able children should be asked to think about the gradient of the lines and whether it is possible to work out a label for the lines.

> Graphs for use with this lesson are in the Resources section (pp. 88–90) and on the CD.

LESSON 5   Shape

This lesson was planned for children in Years 4 and 5 but can be adapted for either younger or older classes. The main focus is to allow the children the opportunity to explore 2D shapes, to play with them and to be able to transfer the physical knowledge into mental knowledge enabling them to picture/visualise the shapes. It is also an opportunity to encourage the understanding and use of appropriate mathematical language when the children discuss and describe both 2D and 3D shapes.

Resources for this lesson can be found in the Resources section and are downloadable from the accompanying CD:

- 'Same/different' sheets 1 and 2 (pp. 91–2)
- 'Different to the rest' sheet (p. 93)
- Triangle sheets (3) (pp. 94–96).

Ideas for 'Visualisation' activities with shape can be found on p. 56.

LESSON 6   Number skills

This lesson allows the children the opportunity to use their thinking processes. The 'Zap it!' game allows them to develop their logical thinking but also encourages creative thinking in deciding which properties could be chosen to eliminate the numbers. There should be a basis of previously taught mathematical concepts and vocabulary. This game makes an ideal way to end a unit on number as it consolidates facts but also stretches the application of knowledge and of course it should be fun. The children themselves will be developing their own questioning skills and the teacher can listen carefully to the types of question used and model some questions that the children could use.

Resources for this lesson can be found in the Resources section and are downloadable from the accompanying CD:

- Five by five grid sheets (4) (pp. 99–100)
- Target Board sheets (p. 101–2)
- 'Zap it' rules (p. 103).

Numeracy lesson plan 2: Multiplication (1)

	Year Group/s: Year 6

Learning objectives/lesson focus:
- Understand the operation of multiplication and the associated vocabulary, and its relationship to addition and division.
- Solve mathematical problems or puzzles, recognise and explain patterns and relationships, generalise and predict. Suggest extensions by asking 'What if ...?'

Targeted language skills:
The children will develop the vocabulary of multiplication through discussion of tasks.

Resources:
Bingo cards, pens, cloths, counters.

Vocabulary:
times, multiply, product, multiple, factor, inverse.

Mental maths: Each pair is given a bingo 'card'. If this is laminated the children can have a pen and cloth, if it is not then the children need counters. The teacher generates numbers from 1 to 100 and the game is played as described on p. 83.

Whole class work: The children are taught the principle of the associative law, e.g. $16 \times 12 = (2 \times 8) \times 12 = 2 \times (8 \times 12) = 2 \times 96 = 192$. More examples are modelled, then the children are asked to work in their groups.

Group activities: Children are given opportunities to develop their knowledge of the associative law to help with multiplication facts. The work is differentiated as follows:

Differentiation: The less able group play with their knowledge of multiplication facts to work out all possibilities for sums, e.g. 6×12: $6 = (2 \times 3)$, $12 = (2 \times 6)$ or (4×3). Discussion should be based on which factors would be most helpful to do the sum. For some children using $2 \times$ (or doubling) would be the choice.
The middle group should work on sums involving decimals, e.g. $9.6 \times 30 = 9.6 \times (3 \times 10) = (9.6 \times 10) \times 3 = 96 \times 3 = 288$. Discussion should focus on whether trying to find the factor 10 helps in solving the sums? What other factor would help and why?
The more able group should explore several examples of sums to come up with some useful rules, e.g. find the factor 2 for doubling; if there is a decimal find a factor 10 to get rid of it, etc.

Plenary: The more able could feed back to the class on the rules that they have found out and the rest of the class could challenge the group to work out sums using their rules. Discussion could follow to see which of the rules are the most useful.

Lesson evaluation:
Were the children engaged during the introduction?
Were they able to participate in the mental maths?
Could they contribute to the discussions using the correct mathematical vocabulary?
Could they solve multiplication problems using the associative law?

Did they work well in their pairs?
Did they complete the task successfully within the time?

Numeracy lesson plan 2 – Multiplication (2)

Before the lesson:

1. Make sure that the resources are prepared with regard to the needs of your class.
2. Share the plans with the teaching assistant.
3. Some children find learning multiplication facts very difficult and for some of these activities those children could be supported by giving them copies of the facts.
4. Other objectives are also covered in this lesson but not included here.

Language

It is very important to use the correct mathematical language but to make sure that the children make the connection that multiplication is actually the same as 'times'.

Vocabulary: multiply, multiplication, times, multiple of, rows of, columns of, sets of.

Resources

Bingo cards need to be prepared in advance. Ideally they can be laminated or just slipped into plastic envelopes. This allows the children to use wipe-able pens and prolongs the life of the cards.

As an extension activity the children may want to use a blank Bingo card and work out which factors they need to get the numbers shown and to guarantee a win!

Questioning/thinking

Some children may find the associative law a little difficult and may need more time to 'play' with the idea of the commutative law first using smaller numbers and cubes or rods, e.g. how many ways can you sort 12 out into equal rows/columns without a cube left over? (One row of 12 or 12 rows of 1; two rows of 6 or 6 rows of 2; 3 rows of 4 or 4 rows of 3, etc.)

It is important to focus the children on the patterns they are finding rather than simply pushing the knowledge of multiplication facts, and if this knowledge is restricting the thinking and exploring, then there is no harm in giving them calculators initially to support them in the search.

Learning Objectives/lesson focus		Year group
Targeted language skills		
Resources	Vocabulary	
Mental maths		
Whole class work		
Group activities		
Differentiation		
Plenary		
Lesson evaluation		

Outcomes/assessment

The plenary can be used to assess the more able group. If they can explain to the rest of the class how to work the calculations out then they have obviously understood the concepts.

For the least able the main focus would be on assessing whether they have understood the concept of factors and can find these for several numbers.

The majority of the class would have consolidated knowledge of tables facts which could be tested at a later stage.

Numeracy lesson plan 3: Factors (1)

	Year group/s: Years 5/6

Learning objectives/lesson focus:
- Understand the operation of multiplication and the associated vocabulary, and its relationship to addition and division.
- Solve mathematical problems or puzzles, recognise and explain patterns and relationships, generalise and predict. Suggest extensions by asking 'What if ...?'

Targeted language skills:
The children will develop the vocabulary of multiplication through discussion of tasks.

Resources
Multiply and divide loop cards, large version of multiplication square for whole class and smaller ones for pair work; 'complete the multiplication grid' sheet; 'Which table am I?' sheet.

Vocabulary:
times, multiply, product, multiple, factor, inverse.

Mental maths: The children will work through the Multiply and Divide loop cards.

Whole class work: Using the large version of the multiplication square the teacher shows the class a number, e.g. 45, and asks, 'Which column or row do you think this will fit into?' Answers should be encouraged that develop understanding of factors and multiple rules (e.g. all numbers in 5 times table end in 0 or 5). Teacher also needs to ask whether the number can go into any other position in the square. This should develop the children's understanding of the commutative law, (e.g. $9 \times 5 = 5 \times 9$)

Group activities: Children work on developing their knowledge of multiplication facts and the relationship between multiplication and division. The work could be differentiated as follows:

Differentiation: Less able group – using a blank multiplication square the children can fill in the missing square, making sure that they use a different colour to write in the commutative multiple, e.g. $5 \times 9 = 45$ can be in one colour and $9 \times 5 = 45$ can be in a different colour. This will then allow the children to realise that not all the tables have to be learnt: once some are known it is easy to find out others. Using the coloured-in square, the children can work out how many tables' facts they actually need to learn.
Middle ability group – using the 'complete the multiplication grid' sheet the children have to work out the missing numbers. Discussion should focus on how knowledge of division facts helps with working out the answers.
More able group – using the sheet which table am I?' the children have to work out the value for the letters and then the tables facts and work out a new one themselves.

Plenary: Ask the children what facts would help in solving these types of questions.
$?? \times ? = 325$ $?? \times ?6? = 1638$ $?2? \times ?? = 9454$

Lesson evaluation:
Were the children engaged during the introduction?   Did they work well in their pairs?
Were they able to participate in the mental maths?   Did they complete the task successfully within the time?
Could they contribute to the discussions using the correct mathematical vocabulary?   Did they show their understanding of the commutative law?

Numeracy lesson plan 3: Factors (2)

Before the lesson:

1. Make sure that the resources are prepared with regard to the needs of your class.

2. Share the plans with the teaching assistant.

3. Some children find learning multiplication facts very difficult and for some of these activities those children could be supported by giving them copies of the facts, but avoid the use of these early in the lesson.

4. Other objectives are also covered in this lesson but not included here.

Language

It is very important to use the correct mathematical language but to make sure that the children make the connection that multiplication is actually the same as 'times'.

Resources

The loop cards can be used as a group activity for the lower ability if they struggled with the mental starter. They could use them as they would dominoes.

The blank multiplication square could be displayed on a whiteboard.

Questioning/thinking

The main focus of this lesson is to allow the children the opportunity to find the patterns in tables' facts. This knowledge will help them in learning and applying these facts in their maths work. Questions should always be directed at helping them get to the answer themselves, e.g. with the 'Which table am I?' sheet questions could be 'What do you notice about the first three numbers?' Single digits. 'So what can this mean about the multiple?'

Also, when working on the 'Which table am I?' sheet it is important to instil in the children that letters are not always arranged so that $A=1$, $B=2$, $C=3$, etc. This will help them greatly when they move on to more formal algebra.

Learning Objectives/lesson focus		Year group
Targeted language skills		
Resources	Vocabulary	
Mental maths		
Whole class work		
Group activities		
Differentiation		
Plenary		
Lesson evaluation		

Outcomes/assessment

The main assessment opportunities for the three groups would be:

Less able group – do the children now find that the learning of the tables facts is not as daunting, as knowledge of some facts will help them know other facts (commutative law)?

Average group – do they understand the relationship between multiplication and division?

More able group – can they recognise and explain patterns?

Numeracy Lesson Plan 4: Handling data (1)

Learning objectives/lesson focus: Handling data

	Year group/s:
• Solve a problem by collecting, organising, representing, extracting and interpreting data in tables, graphs and charts. • Solve mathematical problems or puzzles, recognise and explain patterns and relationships, generalise and predict. Suggest extensions by asking 'What if ...?'	Years 5/6

Targeted language skills: The children will develop the vocabulary of handling data through analysing and creating graphs.

Resources: Resource sheets – Graph 1, Happy/sad graph, Food intake graph.	**Vocabulary:** line graph, data, interpret, x-axis, y-axis, horizontal, vertical, diagonal.

Mental maths: Use a large version of Graph 1 (or display on whiteboard). Make sure the children understand that what they are seeing is a graph which represents a set of continuous data. Discuss what the x-axis and the y-axis could be. Allow them to discuss this in pairs, then take some answers. Choose a couple of examples and ask the children to explain how the graph is representing the data, e.g. one example might be the temperature against time (day or year). Ask them to consider what each section of the graph is telling them: Why is the line going up? What is the lowest value on the y-axis? What could the values be on the x-axis? Where would be the highest temperature on the graph? The lowest?

Whole class work: Using their ideas from the mental maths introduction they need to annotate their graphs, showing what it is representing for their choice of variables.

Group activities: The children need to continue to focus on interpreting information from a line graph.

Differentiation: Less able group: using the happy/sad graph go through a well-known story such as a fairy tale and plot how the characters feel, e.g. for the Three Little Pigs story plot how the first pig feels with completion of his house, then when the wolf blows it down, when he stays with the second pig, when that house is blown down, etc. Change the emphasis and plot the graph for another character in the story; in this example it could be the wolf. Compare graphs. What do you notice?
Middle ability group: using the food intake graph ask the children to plot their food intake for the last 24 hours and compare with other children. What do they notice? Similarities, differences.
More able group: using graph paper ask the children to plot the multiples of 2 – what do they notice? Then on the same graph plot multiples of 4, then 8. What do they notice about the lines? Could they predict what sort of line the multiples of 16 will be? Or 0.5?

Plenary:
Using the happy/sad graph ask the children to plot how they felt during this session. Some need to explain their graphs to the class.

Lesson evaluation:

Were the children engaged during the introduction? Were they able to participate in the mental maths? Could they contribute to the discussions using the correct mathematical vocabulary?	Did they work well in their pairs? Did they complete the task successfully within the time? Could they interpret the graphs?

Numeracy lesson plan 4: Handling data (2)

Before the lesson:

1. Make sure that the resources are prepared with regard to the needs of your class.
2. Share the plans with the teaching assistant.
3. Data handling can be very difficult for some children to understand as it involves the representation of facts in a diagrammatic way. They therefore need to be led through the process carefully and basic transferring of data onto graphs needs to have already been covered.
4. Other objectives are also covered in this lesson but not included here.

Language

It is very important to use the correct mathematical language, especially with regard to the labelling of axes. Some children will also find the terms 'vertical', 'horizontal' and 'diagonal' difficult to grasp. Some kinaesthetic activities involving body movements would help here and could be reinforced in PE lessons, e.g. lie down horizontally, stand up as vertically as you can, move across the room diagonally.

Questioning/thinking

Encourage the children to relate what they can see on the graph to what is actually happening. Explain that this is a visual representation of the data/information.

Questions should always be directed at helping the children to relate the positive slope to something increasing and the negative slope to something decreasing. Questions as to the labelling of the axes and why it is important that this is standardised will help with their understanding:

'What would have happened to our graph if the gaps between the points were not the same?'

'Would we be able to understand it as clearly?'

'Think about the gradient of the lines – is it possible to work out a label for the lines?'

Resources

The resources supplied for this lesson are only examples and many other graphs can be used, even those produced by a previous class working on data handling.

You may also want to consider having larger apparatus available, either for this lesson or for others on the same theme, e.g. a rope can be used in a large space to produce the line in a graph drawn on the floor; data could be plotted using quoits and linked by the rope.

Outcomes/assessment

The main assessment opportunities for the three groups would be:

Less able – can they tell you what is happening to the emotions simply by interpreting one of the happy/sad graphs?

Average group – using only their food intake graphs could they tell you when they ate and which meal was the largest?

More able group – this group might even be able to start expressing some sort of relationship between the gradient and the value of the line, from simply stating that the greater the 'jumps' the steeper the line to actually working out the relationship Y = 2 ×, etc.

Learning Objectives/lesson focus		Year group
Targeted language skills		
Resources	Vocabulary	
Mental maths		
Whole class work		
Group activities		
Differentiation		
Plenary		
Lesson evaluation		

Numeracy lesson plan 5: Shape (1)

	Year Group/s: Years 4/5

Learning objectives/lesson focus: Shape
Describe and visualise 3D and 2D shapes; classify them according to their properties

Targeted language skills: The children will focus on using the correct language related to shape.

Resources: Same/different sheets 1 and 2; 'different to the rest' sheet; triangles sheets (all three).	**Vocabulary:** circle, triangle, equilateral triangle, isosceles triangle, quadrilateral, rectangle, oblong, square.

Mental maths: Visualisation – choose from the suggested examples on p. 56.

Whole class work: Using the 'same/different' sheet ask the children to come up with suggestions of what a circle and a quadrilateral have in common and why they are different. Accept all factual answers, e.g. they may say that the similarities are that they are shapes, they are 2D, etc; some differences mentioned will probably relate to sides. Now use an equilateral triangle and a square to compare and contrast. Move on to the 'different to the rest' sheet (see notes in Chapter 7).

Group activities: The children will be given the opportunity to explore properties of 2D shapes.

Differentiation: Less able group: using a variety of straw lengths, representing sides and connectors, the children are to create different triangles and note the properties of the triangles created. If there is time they could move on to quadrilaterals.
Average group: this group will use the 'different from the rest' sheet and choose three quadrilaterals to compare and contrast.
More able group: using the isosceles, right-angled and equilateral triangle templates, the children should explore what shapes can be created when you combine two triangles. They need to identify the shapes and list the properties. They could then move on to seeing whether they can recognise any patterns to link the shape created to the triangles used in its creation.

Plenary: One possibility is to get one of the groups to feed back to the rest of the class, asking them to explain any patterns they have noticed. An alternative would be to move them on to considering 2D shapes as faces of 3D shapes and using templates ask them what shapes could be created by, for example, equilateral triangles. Would you need other faces to complete the 3D shape?

Lesson evaluation:
Were the children engaged during the introduction?
Were they able to participate in the mental maths?
Did they complete the task successfully within the time?
Could they recognise the properties of the shapes used?

Did they work well in their groups?
Could they visualise the shapes?
Could they contribute to the discussions using the correct mathematical vocabulary?
Did they recognise any patterns?

Numeracy lesson plan 5: Shape (2)

Before the lesson:

1. Make sure that the resources are prepared with regard to the needs of your class. The triangle templates all need to have a side of the same length.

2. Share the plans with the teaching assistant.

3. Children will need to have had an introductory lesson into naming 2D shapes and a brief summary of their properties. This lesson focuses on the children exploring the shapes and understanding what the properties actually relate to.

4. Other objectives are also covered in this lesson but not included here.

Resources

It is vitally important for children who are working on shape to have some apparatus to work on. Many companies produce smart colourful shape templates but simple card cut-out would also suffice.
The sheets that are used are the compare and contrast ones provided in pp. 91–3.
Visualisation ideas can be found on p. 56.

Language

It is very important to use the correct mathematical language especially with regard to describing shapes.
Allowing the children to learn using the shapes, straws, etc. can help relate the language to its meaning.
Some assistance may be needed in enabling some of the children to learn words such as 'quadrilaterals'.
Linking the new word to something they already know helps a lot: in this example, linking it to a quad bike which has **four** wheels.

Questioning/thinking

The main focus of this lesson is to allow the children the opportunity to explore 2D shapes, to play with them and to be able to transfer the physical knowledge into mental knowledge enabling them to picture/visualise the shapes.
Questions need to be aimed at focusing the children on looking carefully at each shape: What is it that changes a square into a rectangle? Could you make a rectangle out of two squares? How many squares would you need to make another square?
Some of the brighter children should be asked to think about the gradient and how angles affect the probability of creating a shape, e.g. can you have a triangle with two right angles? Why? Can you have a quadrilateral with three equal sides? What are its other properties?

Learning Objectives/lesson focus		
Targeted language skills		
Resources	Vocabulary	
Mental maths		
Whole class work		
Group activities		
Differentiation		
Plenary		
Lesson evaluation		

Year group

Outcomes/assessment

The main assessment opportunities for the three groups would be:
Less able group – they can create 2D shapes and name them, maybe even listing some of their properties.
Average group – they can identify the main properties of 2D shapes and classify them through using the sheets.
More able group – as the other two groups, but considering the relationships of angles and even parallel lines.

Numeracy lesson plan 6: Number skills (1)

	Year group/s: Years 4/5/6

Learning objectives/lesson focus: Problem-solving
Solve mathematical problems or puzzles, recognise and explain patterns and relationships, generalise and predict. Suggest extensions by asking 'What if …?'

Targeted language skills: The children will focus on using the correct language to explain their thought processes when solving a problem.

Vocabulary:
digits, square numbers, prime numbers, factors, multiples, total, product.

Resources
Five by five grid sheets, target board sheets, counters.

Mental maths/Whole class work:
Play the 'Zap it!' Game.
Rules for this are found on, p. 103.

Group activities:
The children will be given activities that test out their ability in recognising properties of number and how to manipulate numbers to solve problems.

Differentiation:
Less able group: complete the five by five grid (5 start). They can use apparatus.
Average group: using the target board for numbers up to 100, answer the questions on the sheet.
More able group: they can have a go at the five by five grid (22 start), then in pairs design their own using the blank grid.

Plenary:
Use one of the created five by five grids to complete as a class.

Lesson evaluation:
Were the children engaged during the introduction?
Were they able to participate in the mental maths?
Did they complete the task successfully within the time?
Did they work well in their groups?
Could they contribute to the discussions using the correct mathematical vocabulary?
Did they recognise any patterns?

Numeracy lesson plan 6: Number skills (2)

Before the lesson:

1. Share the plans with the teaching assistant.

2. This lesson can only be given once the children are relatively confident with some mathematical concepts and vocabulary. It makes an ideal way to end a unit on number as it consolidates facts but also stretches the application of knowledge and of course it should be fun.

3. Other objectives are also covered in this lesson but not included here.

Language

The activities in this lesson, particularly the warm up game 'Zap it!' encourage the children to use correct mathematical language. There is an ideal opportunity here for the teacher to help children refine their maths language.

Questioning/thinking

The main focus of this lesson is to allow the children the opportunity to use their thinking processes. The 'Zap it!' game allows them to develop their logical thinking but also encourages creative thinking in deciding which properties could be chosen to eliminate the numbers.

The children themselves will be developing their own questioning skills and the teacher can listen carefully to the types of question used and model some questions the children could use.

Resources

Very basic resources are needed. You may want to laminate the grids so that children can work out the numbers on the grid as they go along. Answers could then be wiped off and the grids used again. All sheets can be used on the interactive whiteboard. If pupils do not have individual whiteboards they could write on a piece of paper.

Learning Objectives/lesson focus	Year group
Targeted language skills	
Resources	Vocabulary
Mental maths	
Whole class work	
Group activities	
Differentiation	
Plenary	
Lesson evaluation	

Outcomes/assessment

This lesson gives several opportunities for assessment. You may want to focus on one group and check their skills with calculation, for example, as they go through the grids. Alternatively you may want to listen carefully to the types of question the children ask of one another, or assess which children are aware of what prime numbers are, etc. Do they use that term in their questioning? Do they recognise that their number is a prime number?

7 Starters and plenaries

Thinking activities are ideal for warming up before a lesson or to set the scene for a maths or literacy session. The plenary is an opportunity to share ideas and information related to the work covered and could incorporate one of the short thinking games suggested in this chapter. These could also be used as a 'brain break' to give the class an opportunity to change pace and use their brains in a different way.

????? Questions ?????

Provide the children with an 'answer' and in groups they should work out 5 possible questions that could be answered by this word. They can then share their questions and answers with the rest of the class.

Example: answer – 'pencil'
Question 1 – What do you use to write with?
Question 2 – What is long and thin, made of wood, and you use it at school?
Question 3 – What are you always losing at school?
Question 4 – You use it to make marks that can be rubbed out – what is it?
Question 5 – The more you use it the shorter it gets – what is it?

Other suggested 'answer' words:
bread, house, horse, the Queen, chair, number 10.

Lists

Divide the class into groups of 4 or 5 and ask them to come up with a list of 10 things:

- that a spaceman might take with him on a flight to the moon.

or

- that a pirate might have in his sea chest.

or

- that an alien might bring with him to earth.

I-spy

Divide the class into groups. Look around the classroom – how many things can you see that are made of...

wood?
plastic?
paper?

Alphabet... A, B, C, D, E, F, G, H, I, J,

Provide groups of children with the blank alphabet sheet (there is one provided on p. 106) and give them 5 minutes to think of things that they would find around the school beginning with each letter.

K, L, M, N, O, P, Q, R, S, T, U, V, W, X, Y, Z.

Empty boxes

This is a well-known activity to help children with place value. You can make it as hard or easy as you want to by changing the number of boxes and by changing the types of answer you want. This example is the easiest version:

- You need a sheet with two empty boxes like this:

- The children generate digits from 0 to 9 (using dice, cards, etc.). The aim is to create the largest number or the smallest number by placing the digits in the appropriate boxes.

This can be developed into a game for 2–4 players where each child in turn tries to create their largest or smallest number.

The game can be made more difficult by increasing the number of boxes to include hundreds and thousands or to introduce decimal places.

It can also be made more difficult by asking the children not to produce the largest number but the second largest or the second smallest.

Guess my number

This is another well-known game and can be played between the teacher and the class or between a child and a class or in pairs.

The aim is for the children to guess what the number is, using the least number of questions. They have to ask questions which have only 'yes' or 'no' as answers.

It is very easy to differentiate this game by restricting the possible numbers to make it easier and extending the range, maybe to include decimals or fractions, to make it harder.

It can also be modified to 'Guess my shape' where the children ask about the properties of a shape to find out which one it is.

More lists

How many things can you think of that...

- are red?
- rhyme with 'day'?
- you can put things in?
- begin with 's'?
- you would find on the beach?
- you have under your bed?

Tell your partner...

What you did when you got up this morning...? make sure it is in the correct sequence!

or

How you make a sandwich?

▨ Visualisation

This is a great way to assess whether the children have truly understood the properties of a shape. However there are two groups of children who will find this activity particularly difficult. The first group are the children who struggle with the language of shape, and the second group are those who find visualisation of any type difficult to do and therefore need support in developing their visualisation skills. The first group need to be supported in their learning of names and linking the names to shapes. Flash cards are a simple way to do this but they should be supported by auditory input. The children need to hear the name when they see the word and the shape. The second group are much harder to support. They will need a lot more practice in drawing the shapes so that they use their kinaesthetic learning skills as well as their visual and auditory ones. Some of this latter group may never be able to visualise and you must therefore ensure that they can actually draw the shapes when doing the activities. But be careful that the rest of the class do not use their drawings as a sneaky support to their visualisation!

Here are some examples of visualisation ideas that can also be used with the sample lesson on shape in Chapter 6:

1. **Visualise a square.**
   Think of a diagonal line cutting the square into two triangles.
   Draw and name one of the triangles formed.

2. **Visualise a square.**
   Cut the square along a diagonal line.
   Move the triangles formed and line them up, one side against an equal side.
   Draw the shape you have made.

3. **Visualise a rectangle.**
   Cut the rectangle along a diagonal line.
   Using the triangles formed line them up, one short side against another short side.

4. **Visualise a rectangle.**
   Cut the rectangle along a diagonal line.
   Using the triangles formed line them up, one long side against another long side.

5. **Visualise a square.**
   Place an equilateral triangle (which has the same length sides as the square) on to one of the sides of the square.
   Cut the shape formed along its line of symmetry.
   Draw the shape formed.

Have fun with making up your own.

Same and different

This is such a simple idea but the children through participation in this activity focus clearly on the details of concepts. At its simplest, it involves the children focusing on two ideas. We have included some examples here to help explain what the children could come up with and how that benefits them in their learning.

Example 1: the numbers 4 and 9

Same	Different
They are both under 10. They are more than 3. They are one-digit numbers. They are square numbers. They are 1 less than a multiple of 10.	One is odd and one is even. One is in the three times table, one in the two times. One is more than 5, the other is less than 5.

As the children come up with the answers it is the perfect opportunity for assessment. The type of answer the child comes up with will reflect their level of understanding of number. The child who said 'They are more than 3' is obviously at a different level of understanding to the child who said 'They are 1 less than a multiple of 10.'

Example 2:

Same	Different
They are shapes. They have sides. The sides are straight. There are more than two sides. There are corners. They are 2D shapes.	One has three sides, the other four. Different number of corners. One has right angles. Different number of lines of symmetry. Perimeters are different.

The teacher can work on the answer and develop the children's learning further.

Variations

This activity can be developed to look at three different things. This can be a precursor to grouping activities.

See also the lesson plans Literacy A and Numeracy 5 in Chapters 5 and 6 with longer activities based on this theme.

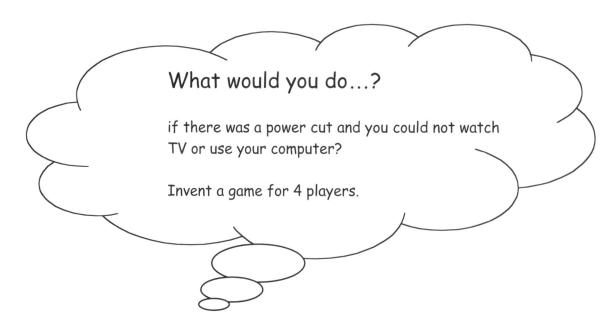

What would you do...?

if there was a power cut and you could not watch TV or use your computer?

Invent a game for 4 players.

Loop Cards

Loop Cards have as many different titles as they have uses. They are simply a 'questions and answer' chain. One card starts the chain off with a question and another card has the answer and another question; this follows through as many cards as you want and ends up with the start card. The cards are distributed to the children and the first person asks the question on their card. The person with the answer stands up and then asks the next question, and so on until the loop is completed. The children need to listen carefully, think what questions might match their answer and keep alert.

Here is a small loop to demonstrate the principle, with various types of question to trigger ideas:

7	3	25	4	16	9
How many sides does a triangle have?	What is five times five?	How many right angles are there in a square?	What is half of 32?	What is the next square number after 4?	What is one less that half of 16?

Questions can be as varied as your imagination allows them to be. They can be simple addition or subtraction calculations, questions from a particular multiplication table, number bonds, etc. or you can have questions and answers based on a history, science or geography topic.

Variations

■ Children could use these cards as a whole class or in smaller groups. They could also use them as dominoes. The following may help in understanding how they can do this:

Use the blank 'Loop Card' template in the 'Resources' section (p. 69) to create your own cards.

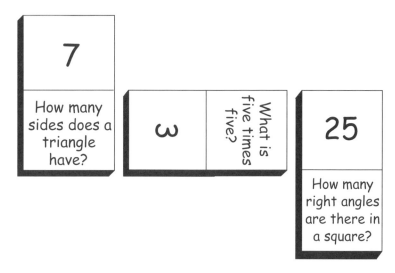

Bingo

Simple rules for Bingo

- Each child or pair should be given a bingo card with a range of answers.
- Cards all need to be different.
- A 'caller' chooses randomly one of the possible answers and announces it to the group.
- The child marks off/covers this if it appears on his/her card.
- This is repeated until one horizontal line is covered and the child with this covered line calls out 'line'.
- This is checked and, if correct, the caller explains to the group which line is now already claimed (top, middle or bottom) and the game carries on until each horizontal line has been claimed.
- When all the answers on one card are covered the person shouts 'house'.

(There are samples of Bingo Cards in the Resources section on pp. 78–82 and on the accompanying CD.)

Variations

- The answers do not have to be numbers; they can be shapes, angles, etc.
- Instead of the whole class working together, bingo could be played with a smaller group.
- The number of possible answers on the card could be increased or decreased.
- Children could make their own cards.

square	pentagon	rhombus
triangle	octagon	trapezium
rectangle	hexagon	circle
parallelogram	heptagon	polygon

Conclusions

By helping children to develop their language skills through thinking activities, you are encouraging them to be active participants in their own learning. The strategies that are taught – visualising, questioning, sharing information, waiting time, role play, cooperation, making connections, investigation, feeding back, etc. – are valuable for developing general problem-solving skills, encouraging children to think for themselves and to apply their knowledge and reflect on their findings. They also cover many of the approaches involved in developing pupils' speaking and listening skills.

Children are taught, not only to answer questions, but to ask them as well and in doing so they embark on a shared adventure of exploration. This makes the curriculum an exciting and challenging place to be, where there are lots of possible answers and making mistakes is a way of finding things out rather than a sign of failure. The 'thinking' classroom is a place where both children and teachers are learners, sharing the need to find out more and the excitement of discovery.

As teachers, you can develop your own questioning skills so that they focus, stimulate and extend thinking and lead to a climate of 'enquiry' within the classroom.

> A Community of Enquiry is achieved when any group of people act co-operatively in the search for understanding. Not only does each member benefit from the ideas and experience of everyone else, each person feels a valued part of the community... This sense of community has a dual aspect: a rational structure for effective thinking and shared ideas, and a moral structure of mutual respect and shared values.
>
> (Fisher 1997)

We have brought together a variety of lesson plans and ideas to help you to incorporate thinking into your own planning and to help children to learn how to learn. This is one of the greatest gifts you can offer, preparing children for the everyday challenges that they will encounter by helping them develop the language skills and the thinking strategies to identify and resolve problems on their learning journey.

It is our hope that because our approach has been in supplying ideas that can be adapted, this approach to teaching can be applied to the whole of the school curriculum, making learning more fun for everyone.

References and further reading

Anderson, L. W. and Krathwohl, D. R. (eds.) (2001) *A Taxonomy for Learning, Teaching and Assessing: A revision of Bloom's taxonomy of educational objectives.* New York: Longman.

Arts Council (1992) *Guidance on Drama Education.*

Assisting Numeracy: A handbook for classroom assistants (1998). BEAM.

Costa, A. and Kallick, B. (2000) *Habits of Mind: A developmental series.* VA: Association for Supervision and Curriculum Development.

Chinn, S. J. and Ashcroft, J. R. (1993) *Mathematics for Dyslexics: A teaching handbook.* Thomson Learning.

Clay, Marie M. (2002) *An Observation Survey of Early Literacy Achievement,* 2nd edn. London: Heinemann.

De Bono, Edward (1993) *Teach Your Child How To Think.* Harmondsworth: Penguin.

DfEE (1999) *Mathematical Vocabulary.*

DfES (2004) *Excellence and Enjoyment: A strategy for primary schools.* Nottingham: DfES.

Fisher, Robert (1997) *Games for Thinking.* Oxford: Nash Pollock Publishing.

Gesell, A. (1966) *The First Five Years of Life.* London: Methuen.

Goodlad, J. I. and Sizer, T. H. (1984) *Changing School's Expertise in Education.* Eric Digests ED345866 (Internet).

Line, Antoinette (1997) *Drama Lessons in Action.* Twickenham: Dramatic Lines.

Morris, Desmond (1967) *The Naked Ape.* New York: McGraw-Hill.

Nash, M., Lowe, J. and Palmer, T. (2002) *Language Development.* London: David Fulton Publishers.

Piaget, J. (1959) *The Language and Thought of the Child.* London: Routledge.

Postman, Neil and Weingartner, Charles (1975) *Teaching as a Subversive Activity.* New York: Dell.

Prashnig, B. (1998) *The Power of Diversity.* London: David Bateman Ltd.

RSA (1998) *Redefining Work.*

RSA (1999) *Opening Minds – Education for the 21st Century.*

Resources for Literacy and Numeracy Lessons

These resources are also downloadable from the accompanying CD

Comparisons

You will need 2 different books

The books I have chosen are:

1. .... by ....

2. .... by ....

Same	Different

Name:

Date:

Comparing books

The books I have chosen are:

1. .... by ....

2. .... by ....

Write *the same* or *different* to complete these sentences about your two books:

The shape of the books is ....

The size of the books is ....

The authors are ....

The titles are ....

The illustrations are ....

The characters are ....

The settings are ....

The number of pages is ....

The price of the books is ....

The size of the font is ....

Name: Date:

Comparing books

same/different	price
similar	information
more/less	fiction
bigger/smaller	non-fiction
thicker/thinner	audience
author	cover
illustrator	blurb
illustrations	title
pages	style
contents	paper
index	card
chapters	softback
font	hardback
prose/poetry	coloured
rhyme	setting
barcode	character

Numeracy Lesson 1: Decimal maths (1)

Add and subtract vocabulary cards

sum	add
increase	total
minus	subtract
difference	decrease

Target Board for calculations to 100

40	45	28
73	33	18
68	37	55
14	72	60

23
39
27
49

Blank Loop Cards

One-place decimal Loop Cards (1)

3.3	One and no tenths

1.0	Four tenths

0.4	Six and six tenths

6.6	Twelve and one tenths

12.1	Three tenths

0.3	Five tenths

0.5	Ten and five tenths

10.5	No units and no tenths

One-place decimal Loop Cards (2)

0	Thirteen and three tenths

13.3	Two and nine tenths

2.9	Four and six tenths

4.6	Eleven and no tenths

11.0	Two and eight tenths

2.8	Ten and two tenths

10.2	One and seven tenths

1.7	Seven and six tenths

One-place decimal Loop Cards (3)

7.6	Six and seven tenths

6.7	Twelve and three tenths

12.3	Nine and three tenths

9.3	Three and seven tenths

3.7	Twelve and no tenths

12.0	Six and four tenths

6.4	One and one tenth

1.1	One tenth

One-place decimal Loop Cards (4)

0.1	Two tenths

0.2	Nine tenths

0.9	One and three tenths

1.3	Eight tenths

0.8	Two and one tenth

2.1	Seven tenths

0.7	Six tenths

0.6	Three and three tenths

Target Board for addition and subtraction

24	53	88	76
71	35	64	45
65	12	82	18
9	27	47	91
			36
			29
			55

Target Board for adding to multiples of 1

3.7	4.5	2.9	6.6	2.8
0.8	5.5	1.5	9.2	8.5
3.4	6.3	7.2	5.6	4.4
7.1	2.4	8.6	0.5	1.9

Target Board for dividing into tenths

0.1	0.1
0.1	0.1
0.1	0.1
0.1	0.1
0.1	0.1

Bingo Cards

Bingo Cards (1)

1	3	4	5
6	7	9	1
2	8	3	2

9	1	7	4
5	3	6	2
7	8	3	4

3	8	1	4
4	5	6	5
7	3	2	9

Numeracy Lesson 2: Multiplication (3)

Bingo Cards (2)

4	9	3	1
7	4	6	5
5	2	8	6

5	8	7	6
1	4	3	9
2	8	5	6

7	5	9	7
8	1	4	2
6	6	3	9

Bingo Cards (3)

7	6	8	3
5	2	1	4
7	9	1	8

5	7	9	6
4	2	9	1
8	8	2	3

3	5	7	9
2	6	8	1
1	4	9	3

Bingo Cards (4)

4	6	9	2
3	5	1	2
7	1	4	8

5	7	2	6
8	5	9	7
3	6	1	4

4	2	7	9
8	3	2	7
6	5	3	1

Bingo Cards (5)

1	3	4	6
5	5	7	7
2	8	9	3

7	1	5	4
4	2	9	3
6	3	8	5

7	9	1	8
4	2	3	3
8	5	6	2

BINGO

Simple rules for bingo

- Each child or pair should be given a bingo card with a range of answers.
- Cards all need to be different.
- A 'caller' chooses randomly one of the possible answers and announces it to the group (or the caller could ask a question which could have its answer on the card).
- The child marks off/covers this if it appears on his/her card.
- This is repeated until one horizontal line is covered and the child with this covered line calls out 'line'.
- This is checked and, if correct, the caller explains to the group which line is now already claimed (top, middle or bottom) and the game carries on until each horizontal line has been claimed.
- When all the answers on one card are covered, the person shouts 'house'.

Variations

- The answers do not have to be numbers; they can be shapes, angles, etc.:

square	pentagon	rhombus
triangle	octagon	trapezium
rectangle	hexagon	circle
parallelogram	heptagon	polygon

- Instead of the whole class working together, bingo could be played with a smaller group.
- The number of possible answers on the card could be increased or decreased.
- The answers could be made easier or more difficult.
- Children could make their own cards.
- The bingo cards could be used for a three-in-a-row game. Please see instructions below.

Complete the multiplication grid

✕		5	7	
		10	14	
4		20		
	48			18
				3

Multiply and divide Loop Cards (1)

12 × 5 27	9 × 3 11	44 ÷ 4 33
49 ÷ 7 42	11 × 3 70	7 × 8 7
6 × 7 60	7 × 11 35	3 × 7 77
27 ÷ 9 21	7 × 5 54	40 ÷ 4 3
10 × 10 56	9 × 6 36	11 × 11 10

Multiply and divide Loop Cards (2)

6×6 5	7×10 8	$48 \div 6$ 9
4×8 121	9×9 100	$12 \div 6$ 32
$60 \div 12$ 81	$45 \div 5$ 12	3×4 63
8×3 2	9×7 4	$28 \div 7$ 6
$30 \div 5$ 64	8×8 30	6×5 24

'Which table am I?'

This is part of one of the tables that you know. Can you work out which digits the letters stand for and which table it is?

H
FE
FH
AE
AH
GE
GH
BE
BH
HE

Make a note of how you worked out the answer.
Were there any patterns that helped you?

Now try this one (remember the letters don't have the same digit value as above!).

G
J
C
EF
EI
EB
FE
FH
FA
GD

Which patterns helped you in this one?
Now you make one like this and test it out on your partner.
Have fun!

Line graph

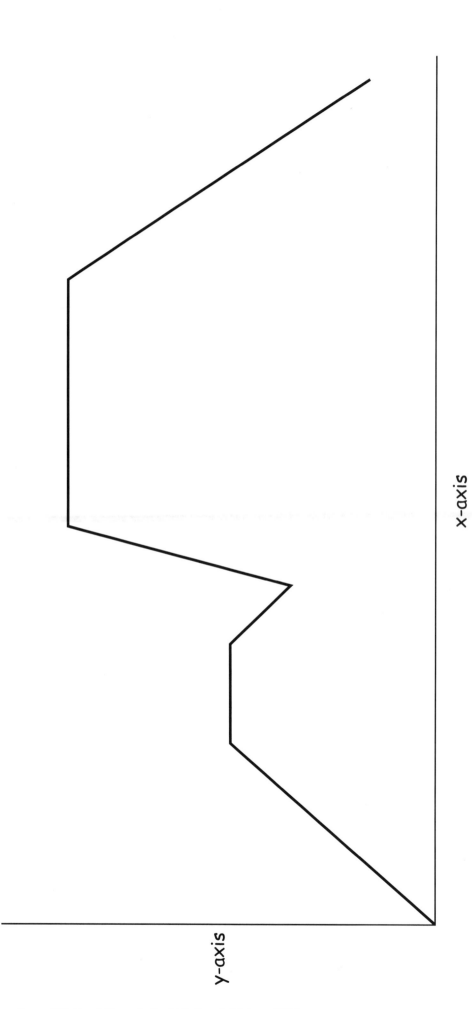

x-axis

y-axis

Happy/sad graph

Very happy

Very sad

Time

Food intake graph

Time

Food intake

Same and different/compare and contrast

Literacy Lesson 5: Shape (1)

Different	Same

Same and different/compare and contrast

Same	Different

Different to the rest

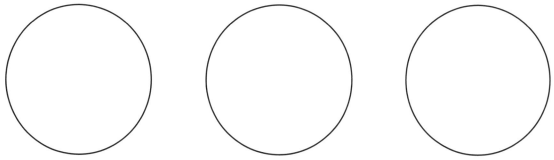

Different to the rest	Different to the rest	Different to the rest
Same		

Equilateral triangles

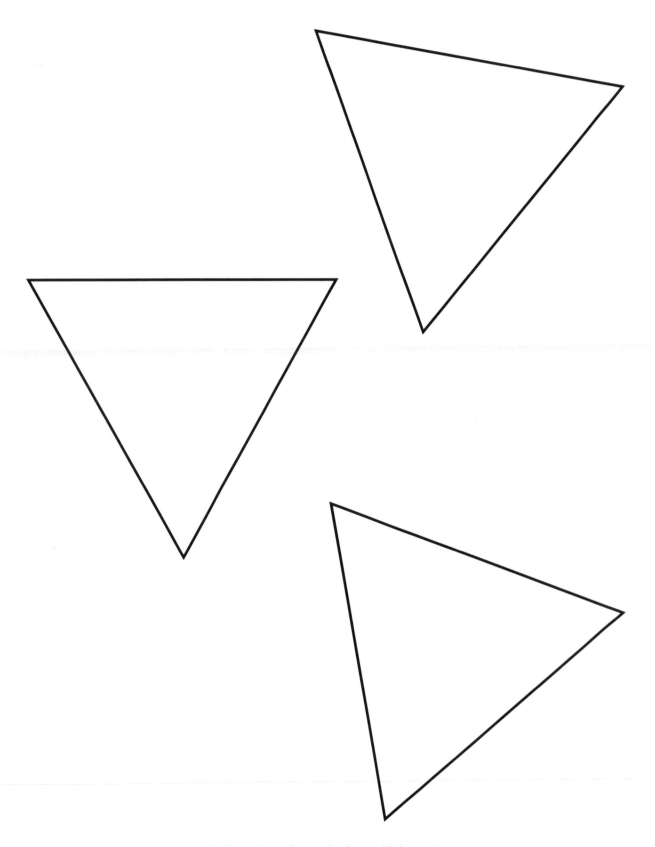

Isosceles triangles

Right-angled triangles

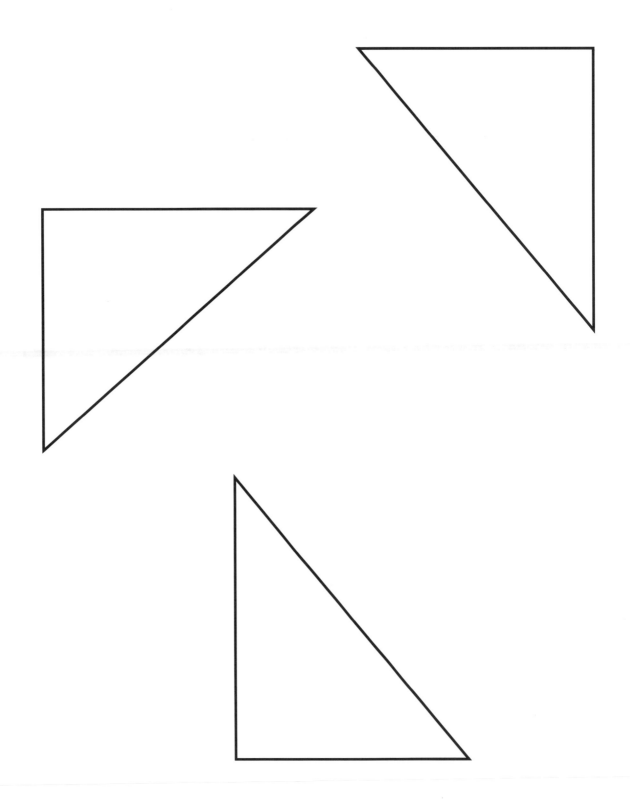

Five by five grid (start at 5)

5	×4	+7	÷9	+6
−1	×4	÷2	+2	×2
−1	÷5	×7	+7	÷8
×2	+3	×4	+4	÷8
+3	×5	−15	+4	÷7

=

Five by five grid
(start at 5: answers)

5	×4 20	+7 27	÷9 3	+6 9
−1 8	×4 32	÷2 16	+2 18	×2 36
−1 35	÷5 7	×7 49	+7 56	÷8 7
×2 14	+3 17	×4 68	+4 72	÷8 9
+3 12	×5 60	−15 45	+4 49	÷7 7

=

Five by five grid (start at 22)

22	×2	+26	÷5	+61
÷3	×10	−45	÷5	+99
×5	÷50	×12	−48	÷6
×8	+16	÷8	+178	×5
−450	÷5	+360	−310	÷8

=

Five by five grid
(start at 22: answers)

22	×2	+26	÷5	+61
	44	70	14	75
÷3	×10	−45	÷5	+99
25	250	205	41	140
×5	÷50	×12	−48	÷6
700	14	168	120	20
×8	+16	÷8	+178	×5
160	176	22	200	1000
−450	÷5	+360	−310	÷8
550	110	470	160	20

=

Target Board for sums 100 with questions

23	28	45	40
39	18	33	73
27	55	37	68
49	60	72	14

Target Board for sums 100 questions

1. Which numbers are greater than 25 but less than 50?

2. Which two numbers make a total of exactly 100?

3. When you double one of the numbers you get 36, which number is it?

4. Write down three ways of making a total of more than 50 but less than 70.

5. Which numbers are multiples of 6?

6. Which numbers have the factors 2 and 5?

7. Find a square number

8. Find a number which is one more than a square number.

9. Which one of the numbers when multiplied by 4 gives one of the other numbers on the board?

10. Which are prime numbers?

Zap it! rules

This can involve as many children as you feel appropriate. The rules are simple:

- The class are each asked to generate a number from 0 to 100. They write these on their whiteboards and make sure none of the other children see the number they have written.
- The teacher then chooses a child to be the first 'zapper'.
- 3–8 children are chosen to stand in front of the class while the zapper moves to a different part of the classroom so that he/she can see all the children.
- The group of children display their chosen numbers by holding the whiteboards in front of them.
- The 'zapper' asks the selected children to arrange themselves either in ascending or descending numerical order.
- The 'zapper' has three zaps to get rid of all the numbers. So he/she has to think carefully of a property of several of the numbers so that more than one child can be zapped. (The choice of even or odd is not allowed and the reason for this should be explained to the class. You may after a few games refuse to accept numbers 'greater than' or 'less than' and again explain the reasons.)
- The 'zapper', depending on age and ability, might choose – in the three times table, a factor of 24, a square number, etc.
- The zapper wins if all the numbers are got rid of (zapped) in three attempts.

> The children gradually get cleverer and cleverer at this game – not just at the 'zapping' but also trying to bring in decimal numbers and factors. You can deal with this as you want to, but remember that all incidents like this are excellent teaching opportunities.

Blank lesson plan (1)

Learning objectives/lesson focus:	NC targets:	Year group/s:
Targeted language skills:		
Resources:	Vocabulary:	
Whole class work:		
Group activities:		
Differentiation:		
Plenary:		
Lesson evaluation:		

Blank lesson plan (2)

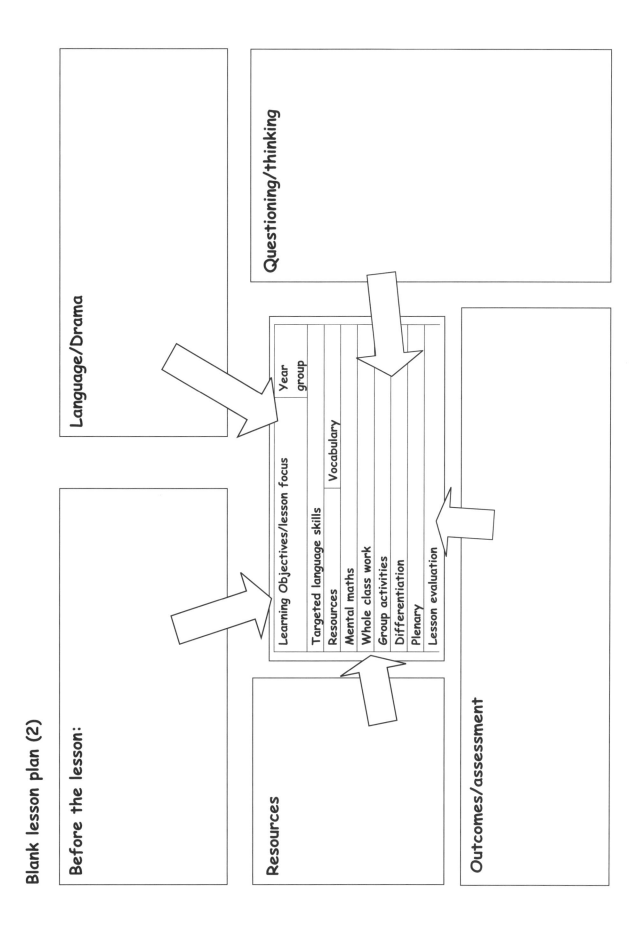

Before the lesson:

Language/Drama

Questioning/thinking

Resources

Learning Objectives/lesson focus		Year group
Targeted language skills		
Resources	Vocabulary	
Mental maths		
Whole class work		
Group activities		
Differentiation		
Plenary		
Lesson evaluation		

Outcomes/assessment

Starters and Plenaries (1)

Name: ....

Write at least one thing that begins
with each letter.

Alphabet
ideas...

The things must be ....

Aa ....   Nn..

Bb ....   Oo ....

Cc ....   Pp ....

Dd ....   Qq ....

Ee ....   Rr ....

Ff ....   Ss ....

Gg ....   Tt ....

Hh ....   Uu ....

Ii ....   Vv ....

Jj ....   Ww ....

Kk..   Xx ....

Ll ....   Yy ....

Mm ....   Zz ....

Three-in-a-row

Playing a three-in-a-row game.

- This is played in pairs.
- The aim is to get three boxes covered in a row before your opponent.
- The rows can be vertical, horizontal or diagonal.
- Opponents can block one another's attempts.
- A set of questions on cards are shuffled and placed face down on the table.
- Each player picks up a card in turn and covers a possible answer, thinking strategically with the aim of getting three answers covered in a row.

Here is an example of a game (player 1 will be circles, player 2 crosses).

Circles player picks a card and decides to cover the nine.

| A square number |

1	3	4	5
6	7	9	1
10	8	3	2

Crosses player picks the next card and covers the three.

| An odd number |

1	3	4	5
6	7	9	1
10	8	3	2

Circles player picks a card and decides to cover the five in the hope of getting a diagonal line.

| A multiple of five |

1	3	4	5
6	7	9	1
10	8	3	2

Crosses player picks the next card and covers the six, planning to get three in a row vertically.

1	3	4	⑤
⨉	7	⑨	1
10	8	⨉	2

A number in the three times table

Circles player picks a card and decides to cover the one, as this now gives two more possible threes in a row.

1	3	4	⑤
⨉	7	⑨	①
10	8	⨉	2

A number when doubled gives an even number

Crosses player picks the next card and covers the seven to block the opponent's attempt at a horizontal line.

1	3	4	⑤
⨉	⨉	⑨	①
10	8	⨉	2

A number between 5 and 10

Circles player picks a card and decides to cover the eight as this now gives a diagonal three in a row.

1	3	4	⑤
⨉	⨉	⑨	①
10	⑧	⨉	2

A number greater than 6

Circles player wins